The War Economy

Echoes of War: The Russia-Ukraine Conflict and Its Global Ripples

SANDEEP CHAVAN

Published by SANDEEP CHAVAN, 2024.

THE WAR ECONOMY

First edition. December 10, 2024.

ISBN: 979-8230391333

Written by SANDEEP CHAVAN.

Table of Contents

To the leaders, policymakers, and organizations tirelessly working to assist war victims and rebuild the economies of nations shattered by conflict.

Your efforts in fostering resilience, creating opportunities, and restoring hope in the face of adversity inspire this work.

And to the global readers—may this book deepen your understanding of the interconnectedness of our world and the shared responsibility we bear in shaping a more equitable and sustainable future.

"In the wake of conflict, economies may falter, but the will to rebuild is unyielding. It is in the resilience of nations and the unity of purpose that we find the blueprint for a better future."

— Sandeep Chavan

Disclaimer

This book is intended for informational and educational purposes only. While every effort has been made to ensure the accuracy and reliability of the information presented, the author and publisher make no representations or warranties regarding the completeness, accuracy, or applicability of the content to specific situations. The insights, data, and opinions expressed in this book are based on research, analysis, and interpretations available at the time of writing and may not reflect subsequent developments.

The content of this book does not constitute professional advice—financial, legal, political, or otherwise—and should not be relied upon as such. Readers are encouraged to consult qualified professionals or conduct their own research before making decisions based on the information contained herein.

Any references to historical events, policies, economic data, or case studies are provided for context and illustrative purposes only. The author and publisher disclaim liability for any errors or omissions and for any consequences arising from the use or reliance on this book's content.

Additionally, while care has been taken to ensure that no proprietary or confidential information is disclosed, the perspectives and interpretations expressed are those of the author and do not necessarily reflect the views of any specific individuals, organizations, or entities mentioned or implied within the text.

This book is not intended to defame, harm, or offend any nation, organization, or individual. Any resemblance to actual persons, living or deceased, or specific events is purely coincidental unless explicitly stated.

By reading this book, you acknowledge and accept that the author and publisher are not responsible for any decisions, actions, or outcomes resulting from its use.

Thank you for engaging with this work with an open mind and a critical perspective.

Preface

The world is transforming at an unprecedented pace. Geopolitical upheavals, economic fragmentation, and technological advancements are reshaping the fabric of global systems. At the heart of this change lies the Russia-Ukraine war, a conflict that began as a regional crisis but quickly evolved into a global disruptor. Exposing vulnerabilities in trade, energy, and supply chains, the war has challenged long-held assumptions about globalization and interdependence. *The War Economy: Global Disruptions from the Russia-Ukraine Crisis* emerges from the need to understand these disruptions, their far-reaching consequences, and the lessons they hold for navigating an increasingly fragmented world.

In this book, I aim to provide a comprehensive exploration of how the war has redefined the global economy. From inflationary shocks and energy crises to trade realignments and the rise of regional powerhouses, the narrative examines the critical themes that define our era. My goal is to go beyond the headlines, delving into the deeper forces at play and offering actionable insights for policymakers, businesses, and individuals alike.

Writing *The War Economy* has been both a challenge and a privilege. The subject's sheer scope required balancing the complexity of global events with presenting them in a manner accessible and engaging for readers. My intention is not only to analyze but also to provide a roadmap for resilience, collaboration, and innovation in the face of uncertainty. Each chapter sheds light on a different facet of this transformation, from the immediate economic impacts of the war to its long-term implications for global stability.

This book incorporates perspectives from experts, case studies, and practical tools to bridge the gap between understanding and application. Appendices provide additional resources, data, and actionable plans, ensuring readers can connect theoretical insights to practical implementation. I hope this format serves as a guide for those seeking clarity in a complex world and empowers readers to take informed steps toward building a more resilient future.

I am deeply indebted to the scholars, professionals, and institutions whose work informed this exploration. Their contributions have been invaluable in shaping the narrative of this book. Above all, this work is dedicated to the global community—leaders, thinkers, and individuals—who navigate today's challenges with resilience and vision.

As you turn these pages, I invite you to reflect on the interconnectedness of our world, the fragility of the systems we depend on, and the opportunities that arise when we rise to meet these challenges. This is not merely a book about conflict or its immediate impacts—it is a broader conversation about how we adapt, evolve, and thrive in the face of disruption.

Thank you for embarking on this journey with me. Together, let us explore the lessons of our time and envision a path forward.

Warm regards,

Sandeep Chavan

Chapter 1: Introduction - A War Economy Emerges

The echoes of war reverberate far beyond the battlefield, reshaping lives, societies, and economies in profound and often unpredictable ways. The Russia-Ukraine conflict, ignited in February 2022, rapidly transcended its regional origins to become a defining moment for the global economy. As missiles rained down on cities and sanctions rippled through markets, the world witnessed a new kind of war economy—one that exposed the fragility of interconnected systems and demanded resilience from nations and individuals alike. This chapter begins with the immediate economic shock of the conflict and unravels the intricate web of global interdependencies that transformed a regional war into a worldwide economic upheaval.

1.1 The Immediate Economic Shock

The outbreak of the Russia-Ukraine war in February 2022 brought an immediate and devastating economic shock that reverberated across both the combat zones and the global economy. As the conflict escalated, its impact on Ukraine's industries and infrastructure, combined with the sweeping sanctions imposed on Russia, created a dual-front disruption that would reshape global trade, energy markets, and financial systems.

The Impact of War on Ukraine's Industries and Infrastructure

Ukraine, often referred to as the "breadbasket of Europe," found its fertile plains and industrial hubs transformed into battlegrounds. Cities like Mariupol and Kharkiv, once thriving centers of manufacturing and commerce, were reduced to rubble. Key industries, including agriculture, steel production, and energy transit, came to a standstill as factories were destroyed, fields became inaccessible, and energy pipelines faced constant threats.

The agricultural sector was among the hardest hit. Before the war, Ukraine was one of the world's top exporters of wheat, corn, and sunflower oil, feeding millions globally. The conflict disrupted planting and harvesting cycles, and blockades in the Black Sea effectively severed Ukraine's access to global markets. Ships laden with grain were stranded in ports, causing food prices to skyrocket and intensifying hunger crises in vulnerable regions like Africa and the Middle East.

Infrastructure destruction compounded the economic fallout. Roads, bridges, power grids, and railways—essential for moving goods and people—were obliterated in the relentless assault. The estimated cost of rebuilding Ukraine's infrastructure soared into hundreds of billions of dollars, leaving the government reliant on foreign aid and loans to maintain even the most basic services.

Russia Under Sanctions: A Forced Recalibration of Global Trade

Russia, the world's third-largest energy producer and a major exporter of commodities such as wheat, fertilizers, and metals, faced a barrage of sanctions from Western nations. These punitive measures targeted its financial institutions, key industries, and political elite, aiming to cripple its economy and pressure the government to withdraw its forces.

The sanctions had immediate consequences. Russian banks were cut off from the SWIFT international payment system, crippling their ability to process transactions with global partners. Multinational corporations from industries spanning technology to retail halted operations in Russia, further isolating its economy. Exports of oil and natural gas, long considered the backbone of Russia's revenue, faced restrictions as European nations sought to reduce their dependency on Russian energy supplies.

This recalibration of global trade forced countries and companies to rethink supply chains and energy policies. European nations, heavily reliant on Russian natural gas, faced soaring energy prices and supply shortages, leading to an accelerated push for renewable energy and diversification of suppliers. Meanwhile, countries like India and China stepped in to purchase discounted Russian oil and gas, reshaping global trade flows and creating new geopolitical alignments.

The immediate economic shock of the Russia-Ukraine war demonstrated the fragility of modern global systems. While Ukraine struggled with the catastrophic loss of industries and infrastructure, Russia grappled with the unintended consequences of its geopolitical ambitions. Together, these disruptions marked the beginning of a war economy that would reshape markets, policies, and priorities worldwide.

1.2 Interconnected Economies: A Global Ripple Effect

In an era defined by globalization, no crisis exists in isolation. The Russia-Ukraine war, though initially confined to Eastern Europe, unleashed economic ripples that spread rapidly across the globe. The interconnected nature of modern economies turned regional devastation into a worldwide crisis, affecting industries, markets, and households far from the frontlines. The war exposed the vulnerabilities of a system where global supply chains, energy security, and food production are inextricably linked.

How Globalization Amplified the Economic Consequences of the Conflict

The interconnectedness of global trade and supply chains magnified the economic impact of the conflict. Before the war, Russia and Ukraine played pivotal roles in the global economy—Russia as a leading exporter of energy and metals, and Ukraine as a major supplier of grains and other agricultural commodities. When the conflict disrupted these outputs, the effects were felt worldwide.

The global nature of financial systems further amplified the economic fallout. Sanctions on Russia froze billions in assets, severed trade ties, and disrupted payment networks, leading to widespread uncertainty in international markets. Nations reliant on Russian and Ukrainian exports scrambled to find alternatives, driving up prices and straining global resources. As one region adjusted its policies to mitigate the impact, the consequences spilled over to others, creating a domino effect of economic disruptions.

Energy Markets in Turmoil: The European Crisis and Global Implications

Europe bore the brunt of the energy crisis triggered by the conflict. Russia supplied over 40% of Europe's natural gas before the war, and sanctions, combined with deliberate supply cuts by Russia, sent prices skyrocketing. Countries like Germany, heavily reliant on Russian energy for industrial production and heating, faced a winter of energy insecurity, prompting governments to ration supplies and subsidize costs for households and businesses.

The energy turmoil extended beyond Europe. Higher natural gas prices drove up electricity costs worldwide, and the scramble to secure alternative energy sources sparked competition in global markets. Developing nations, already struggling with economic instability, were priced out of liquefied natural gas (LNG) markets, exacerbating their energy crises. Meanwhile, oil prices surged as markets adjusted to the reallocation of Russian exports, causing inflationary pressures across industries and raising the cost of living globally.

The crisis also accelerated the push for renewable energy and energy diversification. European nations expedited investments in solar, wind, and nuclear power to reduce reliance on Russian gas, marking a significant shift in global energy policies. While these efforts hold promise for long-term stability, the immediate adjustments have come with significant economic and social costs.

Disrupted Food Supplies: The Far-Reaching Effects on Global Hunger

The war disrupted global food supplies in profound ways, particularly through its impact on Ukraine's agricultural exports. Together, Russia and Ukraine accounted for nearly 30% of global wheat exports, with Ukraine alone providing critical supplies of corn and sunflower oil to markets in Africa, the Middle East, and Asia. The conflict halted shipments from Black Sea ports, leaving millions of tons of grain stranded and pushing food prices to record highs.

The ripple effects were devastating for countries already grappling with food insecurity. In nations like Egypt, Yemen, and Somalia, where Ukrainian grain was a staple, shortages compounded existing hunger crises. The United Nations warned of a looming famine in parts of Africa, while families in wealthier nations felt the pinch of rising food prices in their weekly grocery bills.

Russia's role as a major fertilizer exporter further exacerbated the crisis. Sanctions and disrupted trade flows caused fertilizer prices to surge, reducing agricultural productivity in other parts of the world. Farmers in Latin America and Asia struggled to afford the inputs necessary for their crops, threatening future harvests and perpetuating the cycle of food insecurity.

The global ripple effects of the Russia-Ukraine war underscored the fragility of interconnected systems. Energy insecurity, inflation, and hunger are no longer challenges confined to specific regions—they are global problems requiring global solutions. The conflict revealed the urgent need for diversification, resilience, and collaboration in a world where the fate of one nation is intricately tied to the well-being of many.

1.3 Exposing Vulnerabilities in Global Systems

The Russia-Ukraine war has been a stark reminder of the fragility and interconnectedness of global systems. It exposed critical vulnerabilities in energy and food security, the limitations of just-in-time supply chains, and the challenges faced by economic policies in responding to complex, multifaceted disruptions. These revelations have prompted urgent calls for reform and resilience-building to safeguard against future crises.

Over-Reliance on Singular Sources for Energy and Food

One of the most glaring vulnerabilities exposed by the war is the over-reliance on concentrated sources for critical resources. Europe's dependency on Russian natural gas left it particularly vulnerable when supply chains were disrupted. Before the war, Russia supplied over 40% of Europe's gas, with many countries relying on pipelines that could not be easily replaced by alternative sources. The sudden disruption led to skyrocketing energy prices, rationing, and widespread economic strain, demonstrating the risks of putting too many eggs in one basket.

Similarly, the global reliance on Ukraine and Russia for key agricultural exports highlighted the dangers of concentrated food supply chains. Nations like Egypt, Lebanon, and Bangladesh depend heavily on Ukrainian wheat to meet their food needs, while Russia's role as a leading fertilizer exporter is vital for global agricultural production. The war disrupted these flows, creating shortages and price spikes that left millions on the brink of hunger and economic instability. This dependency has underscored the importance of diversifying trade partners and investing in local production capacities to mitigate risks.

The Fragility of Just-in-Time Supply Chains

Modern economies have long relied on just-in-time supply chains, a system designed to maximize efficiency by minimizing inventory and delivering goods precisely when needed. While cost-effective in stable times, the war exposed how easily this system can crumble under strain.

The conflict disrupted key supply routes across Europe and beyond. Ports in Ukraine were blockaded, rail networks were damaged, and airspace restrictions created logistical bottlenecks. Industries that depended on the seamless flow of materials—such as manufacturing, technology, and retail—saw production delays and rising costs as they scrambled to source alternatives. For example, the auto industry faced shortages of critical components like wiring harnesses produced in Ukraine, halting production lines in Germany and elsewhere.

These disruptions rippled through economies, exposing how the hyper-efficiency of just-in-time models leaves little room for flexibility or resilience in the face of unexpected crises. As companies and governments assess the lessons of the war, there is a growing recognition of the need to build redundancy and buffer stocks into supply chains, even at the cost of higher expenses.

Economic Policies Struggling to Address Multifaceted Disruptions

The war tested the ability of national and international economic policies to respond to overlapping crises. Policymakers found themselves navigating uncharted territory, as the conflict created simultaneous disruptions in energy, food, trade, and financial systems. Central banks, already grappling with inflationary pressures from the COVID-19 pandemic, faced the added challenge of managing soaring energy and food prices driven by the war.

Efforts to contain inflation through interest rate hikes risked slowing economic growth, while subsidies and price caps introduced to shield consumers strained government budgets. The energy crisis in Europe required unprecedented coordination, with countries pooling resources and negotiating joint gas purchases. Meanwhile, developing nations faced mounting debt burdens as they struggled to afford basic imports and subsidies for their citizens.

International financial institutions like the IMF and World Bank stepped in with emergency funding, but their efforts often fell short of addressing the root causes of the disruptions. The war revealed the limitations of existing frameworks in dealing with such multifaceted crises, highlighting the need for more adaptable, forward-thinking economic policies.

The vulnerabilities exposed by the Russia-Ukraine war serve as a wake-up call for governments, businesses, and individuals. Over-reliance on singular sources, the fragility of just-in-time supply chains, and the challenges of addressing interconnected disruptions require systemic changes. The lessons learned from this conflict must inform future strategies, emphasizing diversification, resilience, and the ability to adapt to a rapidly changing world.

1.4 A Catalyst for Change

The Russia-Ukraine war, while devastating, has also acted as a profound catalyst for change. It forced nations, industries, and policymakers to confront their vulnerabilities and rethink global dependencies. The economic disruptions caused by the conflict spurred a reevaluation of priorities in energy security, trade, and resilience, paving the way for more sustainable and diversified systems.

Rethinking Global Dependencies: The Push for Diversification

The over-reliance on singular sources for critical resources such as energy and food has long been a weak point in global systems, but the war underscored just how precarious this dependence can be. European nations, heavily reliant on Russian natural gas, faced a harsh reality when supply lines were severed, leading to soaring energy prices and rationing. This crisis catalyzed an urgent shift toward diversification, as countries sought alternative energy sources and invested in renewable energy to reduce dependence on any single supplier.

Beyond energy, the conflict exposed the need for diversified supply chains in other sectors. Nations that relied on Ukrainian grain or Russian fertilizer found themselves scrambling to secure new suppliers, often at higher costs. This disruption has prompted governments and companies to invest in local production capabilities, foster trade relationships with a wider range of partners, and explore innovations in agriculture, such as vertical farming and alternative fertilizers.

The push for diversification is not merely reactive; it reflects a growing recognition that resilience requires flexibility and redundancy. By spreading risks across multiple sources and systems, countries can better withstand future crises, whether caused by conflict, climate change, or other global shocks.

How the War Economy Reshaped Priorities in Energy, Trade, and Resilience

The economic fallout of the war fundamentally reshaped global priorities, particularly in energy, trade, and resilience. Energy security, once taken for granted by many nations, became an urgent priority as countries raced to secure alternative supplies and reduce reliance on fossil fuels. Europe, for instance, accelerated its transition to renewable energy, increasing investments in solar, wind, and nuclear power. The crisis also revitalized discussions around energy independence, with nations exploring innovative storage technologies and decentralized grids to ensure stability during disruptions.

Trade patterns, too, underwent significant shifts. The war disrupted traditional trade routes and highlighted the risks of concentrated supply chains. In response, countries began reshoring critical industries, such as semiconductor manufacturing, to reduce dependency on distant suppliers. Regional trade agreements gained momentum as nations sought to strengthen ties with neighboring economies and build more resilient networks.

Resilience, both economic and societal, emerged as a central theme. Governments and businesses recognized the need to prioritize long-term stability over short-term efficiency. This shift is evident in the adoption of strategies such as maintaining buffer stocks, investing in infrastructure that can withstand disruptions, and fostering cross-sector collaboration to address complex challenges.

The war economy has left an indelible mark on global systems, but it also offers an opportunity for transformation. By rethinking dependencies, reshaping priorities, and embracing resilience, nations can emerge stronger and better prepared for the uncertainties of the future. While the lessons of the Russia-Ukraine conflict were learned through hardship, they hold the potential to create a more stable and sustainable global economy.

Chapter 2: Energy Crisis: A World in Short Supply

The Russia-Ukraine war unleashed a seismic shockwave across global energy markets, exposing vulnerabilities and triggering an energy crisis that reverberated far beyond the conflict zone. For decades, energy had been a cornerstone of global stability, driving economies, powering industries, and warming homes. Yet, the sudden disruption of oil, natural gas, and coal supplies from two of the world's largest energy players—Russia and Ukraine—upended this delicate balance. Europe, heavily reliant on Russian gas, found itself on the brink of an energy emergency, while nations worldwide grappled with soaring prices, disrupted supply chains, and mounting pressure to rethink their energy strategies. This chapter explores the immediate fallout of the energy crisis, its far-reaching impacts on global markets, and the long-term shifts it has sparked in energy policies and priorities.

2.1 Disruptions to Global Energy Markets

The Russia-Ukraine war sent seismic waves through global energy markets, unraveling supply chains and exposing vulnerabilities that had long been overlooked. This chapter examines how the conflict disrupted energy flows, drove prices to historic highs, and forced nations to reconsider their energy policies and dependencies.

The Shockwaves of War: Energy Prices on the Rise

The onset of the war acted as a lightning rod for global energy markets, driving crude oil prices above $100 per barrel—a level not seen in years—and sending natural gas prices in Europe to unprecedented heights. This price volatility reflected the market's fear of prolonged disruptions to energy supplies, exacerbated by sanctions on Russian exports and damaged transit routes through Ukraine. These factors, combined with a high degree of uncertainty, created an environment ripe for speculation and instability.

The repercussions were swift and far-reaching. Businesses faced skyrocketing energy costs, straining profit margins and forcing energy-intensive industries—such as manufacturing, logistics, and agriculture—to scale back operations. Consumers, meanwhile, grappled with rising utility bills and fuel costs, pushing many households into energy poverty. Governments, already burdened by pandemic-related expenditures, scrambled to introduce subsidies and price controls to shield vulnerable populations, further stretching public finances.

For economies still reeling from the effects of COVID-19, this energy crisis was a sobering reminder of the interconnectedness of modern markets. Disruptions in one region cascaded across the globe, revealing the fragility of energy systems heavily dependent on centralized supply chains. The situation called for a fundamental rethink of global energy policies, emphasizing diversification and resilience to mitigate the risks of geopolitical entanglements.

Supply Chain Interruptions: Oil, Gas, and Beyond

The war also exposed the structural weaknesses in energy supply chains, as both Russia and Ukraine occupy pivotal roles in global energy logistics. Russia, a top exporter of oil, natural gas, and coal, faced constrained trade routes due to sanctions and conflict-related disruptions. Simultaneously, Ukraine, a critical transit hub for Europe's energy supply, suffered extensive infrastructure damage, further choking vital energy flows.

Pipeline disruptions became a symbol of the crisis. Key conduits, such as Nord Stream and others running through Ukraine, were either damaged or deemed unreliable, forcing European nations to seek alternative sources of energy. The closure of Black Sea ports added another layer of complexity, delaying shipments of oil and liquefied natural gas (LNG) and creating bottlenecks that rippled through global markets.

Europe's pivot to LNG as an alternative highlighted the inadequacies of existing infrastructure. With limited LNG terminals and regasification facilities, many nations struggled to meet surging demand. Storage capacities were quickly overwhelmed, and logistical challenges in transporting LNG from producers like the United States and Qatar underscored the gaps in contingency planning. These challenges were not confined to Europe; the interconnected nature of energy markets meant that disruptions in one region reverberated globally, creating fierce competition for alternative resources.

The crisis revealed a stark truth: the global energy system, long reliant on a few dominant players, is alarmingly fragile. This realization has prompted urgent calls for investment in diversified supply chains, resilient infrastructure, and energy independence to safeguard against future shocks.

The Role of Sanctions in Shaping Energy Flows

Sanctions imposed on Russia by Western nations introduced yet another dimension to the energy crisis. These measures aimed to cripple Russia's economic base by restricting its energy exports, blocking access to financial markets, and severing trade ties with key partners. While sanctions sought to weaken Russia's war capabilities, they inadvertently disrupted global energy flows, exacerbating price volatility and supply shortages.

Europe, which had relied heavily on Russian natural gas, oil, and coal, faced the most immediate impact. The sanctions forced a swift and uncoordinated scramble for alternative suppliers. The United States, Qatar, and Norway stepped up energy exports, but existing infrastructure struggled to accommodate the abrupt shift. The transition exposed vulnerabilities in Europe's energy strategy, which had prioritized cost-efficiency over resilience.

Emerging economies, already grappling with inflation and debt, bore the brunt of these disruptions. Wealthier nations outcompeted them for limited supplies, driving up prices and limiting access to critical energy resources. This imbalance intensified global inequalities, as nations with fewer resources faced energy scarcity while developed economies secured their supply chains at premium costs.

Critics of sanctions highlighted their unintended consequences, including heightened inflation and energy insecurity in sanctioning nations. Supporters, however, argued that the measures were a necessary tool to constrain Russia's ability to finance its war efforts. The debate underscored the challenges of balancing strategic objectives with the collateral damage inherent in using economic levers in geopolitics.

In response, nations began to prioritize energy diversification, accelerating investments in renewables, energy storage, and decentralized grids. The crisis served as both a warning and a call to action, emphasizing the need for resilient and adaptive energy policies capable of withstanding geopolitical shocks.

2.2 The European Energy Crisis and Its Global Impact

The Russia-Ukraine war transformed Europe's energy landscape into the epicenter of a global crisis, laying bare the continent's heavy dependence on Russian gas and triggering a scramble for alternatives. This upheaval not only redefined Europe's energy policies but also created cascading social and economic consequences felt across the globe. This section explores Europe's precarious reliance on Russian energy, its search for alternatives, and the ripple effects on households, industries, and emerging economies.

Europe's Reliance on Russian Gas: A Precarious Dependency

For decades, Russian natural gas was a cornerstone of Europe's energy security, fulfilling over 40% of the continent's gas needs. The extensive network of pipelines—including Nord Stream 1 and the Yamal-Europe line—ensured steady and affordable supplies, underpinning the economic stability of major industrial economies like Germany, Italy, and Austria. This dependency was justified by economic pragmatism: Russian gas was abundant, cost-effective, and conveniently delivered, eliminating the need for extensive liquefied natural gas (LNG) infrastructure.

However, the Russia-Ukraine war shattered the assumption that this relationship was secure. The conflict and subsequent sanctions on Moscow weaponized energy supplies, as Russia restricted or halted gas flows to key European customers. Nord Stream 1 became emblematic of this crisis, with gas flows first reduced and then completely stopped, leaving governments scrambling for alternatives. This abrupt disruption exposed the dangers of overreliance on a single supplier with conflicting geopolitical interests.

The energy crisis hit Europe at a critical time, with the prospect of harsh winters heightening public anxiety. Governments implemented emergency measures such as rationing gas, prioritizing essential sectors, and rapidly filling storage reserves. Industries curtailed operations, citizens faced soaring utility bills, and protests erupted as frustrations mounted. The crisis also laid bare the flawed assumption that economic interdependence with Russia would ensure stability, serving as a cautionary tale about the risks of geopolitical entanglements in critical resources.

The Search for Alternatives: LNG and Beyond

The disruption of Russian gas flows triggered an urgent search for alternative energy sources, reshaping Europe's energy strategy almost overnight. Liquefied natural gas (LNG) emerged as a lifeline, with suppliers like the United States, Qatar, and Australia ramping up exports to meet Europe's soaring demand. LNG terminals in Spain, Portugal, and the Netherlands operated at maximum capacity, while plans for new infrastructure, such as floating storage and regasification units (FSRUs), were expedited to bridge immediate gaps.

However, the shift to LNG revealed significant challenges. Infrastructure for importing and distributing LNG was unevenly distributed across Europe, leaving countries like Germany particularly vulnerable due to their lack of LNG terminals. Germany turned to neighboring nations, such as the Netherlands and Belgium, to access LNG supplies, underscoring the interconnected nature of Europe's energy crisis. These stopgap measures exposed the region's lack of preparedness for such a dramatic pivot.

Financially, the transition placed immense strain on European economies. Global LNG demand surged, driving up prices and intensifying competition for supplies. Households and businesses bore the brunt of this surge, with utility bills skyrocketing and manufacturing costs climbing. Emerging economies, unable to compete with Europe's purchasing power, faced energy shortages, further deepening global inequalities.

Beyond LNG, Europe diversified its energy portfolio by increasing imports from Norway, Algeria, and Libya. Renewable energy investments also accelerated, with solar farms and offshore wind projects gaining momentum.

However, the scale and timeframe required to replace fossil fuels limited the immediate impact of these initiatives. Meanwhile, the reactivation of coal-fired power plants highlighted the complexity of balancing energy security with environmental commitments in times of crisis.

Ripple Effects: Energy Poverty and Industrial Slowdowns

The energy crisis extended far beyond Europe, creating profound ripple effects that highlighted the interconnectedness of global energy markets. Rising energy prices plunged millions of European households into energy poverty, forcing families to choose between heating their homes and affording other basic necessities. Stories of families relying on candles to cut electricity costs or bundling children in layers of clothing to stay warm became stark reminders of the crisis's human toll.

Governments responded with subsidies, price caps, and emergency aid packages to shield citizens from the worst impacts. However, these measures strained public finances already weakened by pandemic-related spending, offering only temporary relief. Structural vulnerabilities in Europe's energy system remained glaringly exposed, emphasizing the need for long-term solutions.

Industries across Europe, particularly energy-intensive sectors such as manufacturing, chemicals, and steel, were hit hard. Skyrocketing energy costs forced many factories to scale back operations or shut down entirely, leading to job losses and supply chain disruptions. Small and medium-sized enterprises (SMEs), already reeling from the economic effects of COVID-19, faced existential threats as operating costs became unsustainable.

Globally, the crisis exacerbated competition for scarce energy resources. The surge in European demand for LNG drove up prices worldwide, leaving emerging economies unable to secure affordable supplies. Nations in Africa, Asia, and Latin America faced fuel shortages, inflation, and mounting debt, as energy insecurity deepened existing economic challenges. These cascading effects highlighted the fragility of global energy systems, where disruptions in one region ripple across the globe.

The industrial slowdown in Europe also disrupted global supply chains, particularly in sectors like automotive and electronics. Reduced production led to shipment delays and higher costs for businesses worldwide, compounding the economic instability created by the energy crisis.

Lessons from Europe's Energy Crisis

The European energy crisis underscored the urgent need for diversification, resilience, and sustainability in energy systems. It revealed the dangers of overreliance on centralized suppliers and exposed vulnerabilities in global supply chains. The crisis also highlighted the importance of investing in renewable energy, modernizing infrastructure, and building cooperative frameworks to address future challenges.

As Europe navigates the long road to recovery, the lessons learned from this crisis will likely reshape global energy policies for decades. By prioritizing resilience and sustainability, nations can build systems capable of withstanding geopolitical shocks, ensuring a more equitable and secure energy future for all.

2.3 Long-Term Shifts in Energy Policies

The energy crisis ignited by the Russia-Ukraine war has forced a global reckoning with traditional energy policies, ushering in a new era defined by resilience, sustainability, and innovation. What began as a short-term response to supply disruptions has catalyzed a profound transformation in how nations approach energy security, renewable adoption, and infrastructure modernization. This chapter examines the key shifts in energy policies and their implications for a more resilient global energy landscape.

A Push for Renewables: Accelerating the Green Transition

The crisis underscored the urgent need to transition from volatile fossil fuel markets to renewable energy sources. Beyond addressing the existential threat of climate change, renewables emerged as a critical strategy for achieving energy independence and reducing geopolitical risks. Governments, businesses, and communities aligned behind the green transition, recognizing it as both a necessity and an opportunity.

In Europe, bold commitments to renewable energy became central to the crisis response. The European Union's REPowerEU plan exemplified this shift, setting out ambitious targets to drastically reduce reliance on Russian gas by accelerating investments in clean energy. Across the continent, solar installations surged, offshore wind farms gained unprecedented momentum, and green hydrogen projects were fast-tracked to reshape the energy landscape.

Germany pledged to meet 80% of its electricity needs from renewables by 2030, significantly advancing its climate goals. Other nations, such as Spain and Denmark, launched expansive renewable projects, positioning themselves as regional energy leaders. This strategic realignment demonstrated a dual commitment to decarbonization and energy independence, signaling a long-term shift in priorities.

The private sector played a pivotal role in driving this transition. Companies increasingly turned to power purchase agreements (PPAs), securing long-term renewable energy supplies while supporting the development of new projects. Innovations in green technologies, from battery storage to advanced solar panels, attracted significant investment, reflecting a growing recognition that renewables are both economically viable and environmentally imperative.

Grassroots efforts further amplified the momentum. Community-driven solar cooperatives and localized wind projects empowered citizens to participate in shaping their energy futures. Educational campaigns promoting energy efficiency and renewable adoption built public support, fostering a collective vision for a cleaner and more resilient energy landscape.

This rapid push for renewables marked a defining moment in global energy policy. It demonstrated that urgency can accelerate meaningful change, setting a precedent for future transitions. The shift toward clean energy is no longer just a response to immediate challenges—it is a cornerstone of long-term strategies for sustainability, security, and equity.

Redefining Energy Security: Diversification and Decentralization

The energy crisis redefined the concept of energy security, moving away from the traditional focus on stable fossil fuel supplies from dominant producers. Instead, diversification and decentralization emerged as the twin pillars of modern energy resilience, addressing vulnerabilities exposed by overreliance on single suppliers and centralized systems.

Diversification of Energy Sources and Suppliers

The crisis laid bare the risks of depending heavily on a single energy supplier. Europe, previously reliant on Russian gas, led the charge in diversifying imports, forging partnerships with North Africa, the Middle East, and the Americas. Agreements with Algeria and Egypt expanded pipeline connections, while LNG imports from Qatar, the United States, and Australia filled immediate gaps. These efforts reduced geopolitical risks and stabilized energy markets.

Domestically, nations intensified investments in renewable energy projects. Offshore wind farms, solar parks, and geothermal plants were fast-tracked, recognizing the strategic value of self-reliance. France doubled down on nuclear energy as a long-term solution, while Norway expanded its already robust renewable capabilities. Diversification, both geographically and technologically, became essential for reducing exposure to future disruptions.

Decentralization: A New Approach to Resilience

Decentralized energy systems emerged as a critical strategy for enhancing resilience. Unlike centralized grids, which are vulnerable to disruptions from conflict, cyberattacks, or natural disasters, distributed systems localize energy generation and consumption. Community solar projects, microgrids, and localized wind farms empower communities to produce and store their own energy, reducing dependence on large-scale infrastructure.

In Germany, local governments spearheaded community-owned renewable energy projects, enabling towns to achieve energy independence. Microgrids equipped with battery storage ensured uninterrupted power for critical facilities, such as hospitals and schools, even during outages. These systems not only enhanced resilience but also democratized access to clean energy, particularly in rural and underserved areas.

In regions with limited grid access, decentralized systems provided a pathway to energy equity. Off-grid solar systems, micro-hydro plants, and wind turbines brought electricity to remote communities, reducing carbon footprints while fostering development. Countries like India and Kenya showcased innovative approaches to off-grid solar, demonstrating that decentralization can bridge gaps in both resilience and inclusivity.

The combination of diversification and decentralization offered a holistic vision for energy security, balancing geopolitical considerations with the practical needs of communities. Together, these strategies addressed vulnerabilities exposed by the crisis and charted a course for a more sustainable and equitable energy future.

Innovations in Energy Storage and Infrastructure

Advancements in energy storage and infrastructure are revolutionizing the global energy landscape, addressing long-standing limitations in renewable integration and system reliability. These innovations are paving the way for a more sustainable and secure energy future.

Breakthroughs in Energy Storage Technology

Energy storage is essential for overcoming the intermittent nature of renewables. Recent breakthroughs in battery technologies, including solid-state and flow batteries, are transforming the ability to store and deploy renewable energy efficiently. Grid-scale storage systems, like Tesla's Megapack, allow surplus energy to be stored and utilized during periods of low generation, stabilizing renewable power supplies.

Modernizing Energy Infrastructure

The transition to renewables requires infrastructure capable of handling variability and ensuring reliable distribution. Smart grid technologies enable real-time monitoring and optimization of energy flows, integrating distributed resources like rooftop solar and preventing outages. High-voltage direct current (HVDC) lines facilitate efficient long-distance energy transfer, connecting renewable projects to high-demand regions.

Hydrogen's Emerging Role

Hydrogen is gaining traction as a versatile and clean energy carrier. Investments in green hydrogen production, storage, and pipelines are scaling up, offering solutions for decarbonizing industries such as steel, aviation, and shipping. Countries like Germany and Japan are building hydrogen hubs that integrate production with end-use applications, showcasing its potential in a sustainable energy future.

Toward a Sustainable Energy Future

The innovations and policy shifts spurred by the Russia-Ukraine war signify more than a reaction to crisis—they herald a transformative era for global energy systems. By prioritizing renewables, rethinking energy security, and embracing technological innovation, nations are addressing immediate challenges while laying the groundwork for a resilient, equitable, and sustainable future. This evolving energy landscape reflects the power of collaboration and innovation to turn adversity into opportunity, forging a path toward a cleaner, more secure world.

2.4 The Global Energy Landscape Redefined

The Russia-Ukraine war has irrevocably altered the global energy landscape, creating new alliances, redefining trade dynamics, and highlighting the delicate interplay between sustainability and security. As nations confront the immediate fallout and long-term implications, the evolving energy dynamics are reshaping geopolitics, economic strategies, and environmental policies. This redefinition underscores both the vulnerabilities of current systems and the opportunities for transformation.

New Alliances in Energy Trade: Winners and Losers

The disruption of Russian energy supplies has fractured traditional relationships and forced nations to forge new trade partnerships. This recalibration has created distinct winners and losers, reshaping the balance of power in global energy markets while revealing both vulnerabilities and untapped opportunities.

The Rise of New Energy Players

The crisis has elevated nations previously on the margins of global energy markets. The United States emerged as a dominant LNG supplier, stepping in to fill the void left by Russia. U.S. producers ramped up exports to Europe, cementing America's role as a key energy partner. Similarly, Qatar and Australia capitalized on Europe's urgent demand for LNG, solidifying their positions as essential players in the global energy ecosystem.

North African and Middle Eastern countries, including Algeria and Egypt, strengthened their pipeline networks and expanded exports, leveraging their geographic proximity to Europe. Meanwhile, Gulf nations like Saudi Arabia and the UAE increased oil production and diversified into renewable energy investments, enhancing their influence in both traditional and emerging energy markets.

Russia's Shifting Strategy

Under severe sanctions, Russia pivoted its energy exports toward Asian markets, deepening ties with China and India through discounted oil and gas deals. While this strategy maintained revenue flows, it also underscored the risks of over-reliance on a limited buyer base. Logistical challenges, such as the need for new pipelines and ports, further constrained Russia's ability to fully replace lost European markets, highlighting both the resilience and limitations of its realignment.

Challenges for Energy-Dependent Nations

Countries heavily reliant on energy imports, such as Germany and Japan, faced significant economic strain. Germany's dependence on Russian gas prompted urgent investments in renewables, LNG infrastructure, and energy efficiency measures. Japan, grappling with rising LNG costs, accelerated its diversification efforts, expanding nuclear and renewable energy projects to mitigate future risks.

The Geopolitical Implications

The reshaping of energy alliances has far-reaching geopolitical consequences, intensifying divisions while fostering new opportunities for collaboration.

A Divided Energy Market

The bifurcation of global energy trade into Western-aligned and Russia-China-aligned blocs reflects a growing fragmentation in international relations. This division risks entrenching geopolitical rivalries, complicating efforts to address shared challenges like climate change and global energy security.

Opportunities for Collaboration

Despite these tensions, the crisis has spurred innovative partnerships and investments. Europe's diversification efforts have strengthened ties with North Africa, the Americas, and other regions, fostering a more balanced and interconnected global energy market. Such collaborations highlight the potential for shared solutions in navigating an increasingly volatile landscape.

Lessons for Future Resilience: Balancing Sustainability with Security

The energy crisis has delivered critical lessons on the fragility of existing systems and the urgent need for comprehensive reforms. It revealed not only the dangers of over-reliance on single suppliers but also the transformative potential of diversification, innovation, and collaboration.

Diversification as a Pillar of Security

Nations heavily dependent on Russian gas faced immediate and severe consequences, underscoring the need to cultivate diverse energy portfolios. Investments in renewables, nuclear energy, and regional grids are now seen as essential strategies for reducing geopolitical risks and ensuring long-term stability. Europe's rapid pivot to alternative suppliers and domestic energy production exemplifies this shift.

Reevaluating Strategic Reserves

Strategic petroleum reserves and stockpiles played a vital role in cushioning the immediate impact of supply disruptions. However, their limitations prompted a reevaluation of their size, accessibility, and governance. Future preparedness will require more robust reserves capable of sustaining prolonged crises and adapting to changing energy needs.

Balancing Immediate Security with Long-Term Sustainability

The crisis highlighted the tension between short-term energy security and long-term sustainability. Temporary measures, such as increased coal use, addressed immediate needs but raised environmental concerns. Simultaneously, the crisis accelerated investments in renewables, reinforcing the commitment to a clean energy transition. Policymakers must now align short-term solutions with long-term decarbonization goals, ensuring that immediate actions do not compromise environmental progress.

Global Collaboration as a Catalyst for Innovation

The crisis underscored the importance of global cooperation in addressing energy challenges. Cross-border initiatives, such as the International Solar Alliance and hydrogen partnerships, demonstrated the potential of collective action. By pooling resources and expertise, nations can drive innovation, enhance resilience, and create equitable energy systems that benefit all.

Toward a Transformative Energy Future

The redefinition of the global energy landscape represents both a daunting challenge and a unique opportunity. The lessons of the Russia-Ukraine war highlight the need for resilient, diversified, and sustainable energy systems that can withstand geopolitical and market shocks. Through innovation, collaboration, and a commitment to balance, nations have the chance to forge a more secure and equitable energy future. This evolving landscape, shaped by necessity and vision, holds the potential to drive progress and stability in an uncertain world.

Chapter 3: Food Security in Peril

Food security, a cornerstone of human survival, faces unprecedented challenges in the wake of the Russia-Ukraine war. As Ukraine—a nation often referred to as the "breadbasket of Europe"—found its fertile fields disrupted by conflict, the ripple effects have been felt far beyond its borders. From halted grain exports to soaring fertilizer prices, the war has exposed the fragility of global food systems, leaving vulnerable populations at the brink of hunger and deepening crises in agricultural industries worldwide. This chapter delves into how a single conflict has disrupted one of humanity's most fundamental needs, underscoring the interconnectedness of global food supply chains and the urgent need for resilience in the face of uncertainty.

3.1 Ukraine's Role as a Global Breadbasket

The role of Ukraine in the global food economy is not merely significant—it is foundational. Its vast, fertile lands, immense agricultural productivity, and strategic position in international trade have earned it the moniker "the breadbasket of Europe." For decades, Ukraine has been an essential pillar of global food security, supplying critical commodities to nations around the world. However, the Russia-Ukraine war has profoundly disrupted this role, sending tremors through international food systems and exposing the fragility of over-reliance on a single nation for vital agricultural exports.

The Fertile Fields of Ukraine: A Foundation of Global Food Supply

Ukraine's unparalleled agricultural capacity is rooted in its geography. The country boasts over 42 million hectares of arable land, much of it enriched with black soil, or chernozem. This soil, renowned for its fertility, is one of the most productive in the world. Its nutrient-rich composition, combined with a temperate climate and extensive farming expertise, allows Ukraine to produce a diverse range of crops at scale. Generations of farming tradition, bolstered by modern agricultural practices, have enabled the nation to become a global agricultural powerhouse.

Before the onset of the war, Ukraine consistently ranked among the world's top producers of wheat, barley, corn, and sunflower oil. Its agricultural exports supported economies across continents, forming a critical link in global food supply chains. The country's ability to produce and export large quantities of food ensured its position as a cornerstone of food security for millions.

Key Exports: Grains, Oilseeds, and More

Ukraine's agricultural contributions extend far beyond its borders. It has been a dominant exporter of grains such as wheat, corn, and barley, with wheat alone accounting for more than 10% of global exports. These staples are critical for food security in regions such as North Africa, the Middle East, and South Asia, where reliance on imports is high and domestic agricultural production often falls short of demand.

In addition to grains, Ukraine is the world's leading producer of sunflower oil, supplying nearly half of the global market. This product is a key ingredient in food processing and cooking across the globe, making its availability a crucial factor in price stability for many countries. Furthermore, Ukraine is a major exporter of oilseeds, pulses, and livestock feed, all of which play integral roles in agricultural economies worldwide.

Feeding the World: Dependence on Ukrainian Agriculture

The global reliance on Ukrainian agriculture is a testament to its critical role in sustaining food systems. Countries like Egypt, Turkey, and Indonesia depend heavily on Ukrainian wheat to meet their domestic needs. Europe, meanwhile, relies significantly on Ukrainian corn for livestock feed, ensuring the stability of its meat and dairy industries. This dependency is not limited to food security; it extends to the broader global economy, influencing prices, supply chains, and market stability.

The Russia-Ukraine war disrupted this delicate balance, creating a ripple effect that extended far beyond Ukraine's borders. With ports blockaded, transportation routes severed, and large swathes of farmland rendered inaccessible due to conflict, the flow of Ukrainian agricultural exports came to a grinding halt. This disruption triggered a cascade of consequences: grain shortages in importing nations, skyrocketing prices, and widespread fears of hunger in vulnerable regions. Countries heavily reliant on Ukrainian wheat and sunflower oil faced immediate crises, while others struggled to adapt to the sudden gaps in global supply.

The ramifications of these disruptions highlight the interconnected nature of modern food systems. Nations far removed from the conflict felt its impact, as global food markets reacted with price volatility and resource scarcity. Vulnerable populations in food-insecure regions bore the brunt of these challenges, underscoring the devastating human cost of such disruptions.

A Fragile yet Pivotal Role

The upheaval in Ukraine's agricultural sector serves as a sobering reminder of the vulnerabilities inherent in global food systems. Over-reliance on a single nation for critical commodities leaves supply chains precariously balanced, vulnerable to geopolitical shocks and conflicts. As the world navigates the aftermath of this crisis, Ukraine's role as a global breadbasket is more apparent than ever.

Moving forward, the international community faces the dual challenge of supporting Ukraine's recovery while addressing the structural weaknesses exposed by the conflict. Investing in agricultural resilience, diversifying supply chains, and fostering collaboration between nations will be essential to mitigate future risks. Ukraine's fertile fields remain a beacon of hope for global food security, but they also serve as a warning of the urgent need for more sustainable and interconnected food systems.

3.2 Disruptions in Grain and Fertilizer Supplies

The Russia-Ukraine war has upended global food supply chains at an unprecedented scale, laying bare vulnerabilities in the world's ability to maintain agricultural stability during conflict. Its impact has cascaded through grain and fertilizer markets, triggering a crisis that threatens farmers, consumers, and vulnerable populations across the globe.

Supply Chain Collapse: Blockades and Export Restrictions

Before the war, Ukraine's Black Sea ports, including Odessa and Mariupol, were vital conduits for its agricultural exports, enabling the transport of millions of tons of wheat, corn, and sunflower oil to markets in Europe, Africa, and Asia. These ports served as the lifeline of global food supply chains, connecting Ukraine's agricultural bounty with import-dependent regions. However, as conflict erupted, these critical gateways were blockaded, grinding exports to a halt. Shipping routes became battlegrounds, while essential infrastructure—such as railways, silos, and storage facilities—was severely damaged or rendered inoperable.

The impact of these disruptions was felt far beyond Ukraine's borders. Import-dependent nations, particularly in North Africa and the Middle East, scrambled to secure alternative sources of grains and cooking oil, often at exorbitant costs. The crisis was compounded by export restrictions imposed by several nations seeking to protect their domestic food supplies. Countries like Hungary and India limited grain exports, triggering a domino effect of protectionist policies that worsened shortages and created widespread uncertainty in global markets.

These blockades and restrictions revealed the fragile interdependence of global food systems, where disruptions in one region can lead to cascading effects worldwide. Nations heavily reliant on Ukrainian exports were left vulnerable, while the competition for alternative supplies intensified, pushing prices even higher and exacerbating the global food crisis.

Fertilizer Shortages: A Crisis for Global Agriculture

The war has not only disrupted food supplies but has also dealt a severe blow to the global fertilizer market. Both Russia and Ukraine are major players in this sector, with Russia being one of the largest exporters of nitrogen-based fertilizers and essential components like ammonia, urea, and potash. Ukraine, on the other hand, plays a significant role in phosphate production. Sanctions on Russian exports and the halting of Ukrainian production created a perfect storm, leading to acute shortages and unprecedented price hikes.

Farmers worldwide, particularly in developing nations, have struggled to access affordable fertilizers. In regions where agriculture depends heavily on these inputs, the scarcity has forced many farmers to scale back planting or resort to less effective substitutes, reducing yields and jeopardizing food production. Smallholder farmers in Africa and Asia, already operating on thin margins, have been hit hardest, risking a domino effect of reduced harvests and increased hunger in the coming seasons.

The fertilizer crisis also underscores the interconnected nature of agricultural systems. The lack of inputs in one part of the world impacts food availability and prices globally, creating a ripple effect that compounds the already dire situation in regions vulnerable to food insecurity.

Price Volatility: The Economic Impact on Farmers and Consumers

The war has driven extreme volatility in global grain and fertilizer markets. Wheat prices surged by over 50% in the months following the conflict's outbreak, while fertilizer prices tripled in some regions. For farmers, this volatility has created an environment of uncertainty and rising costs, threatening the sustainability of their operations. High input costs, combined with fluctuating crop prices, have forced many farmers to make difficult decisions, such as planting fewer crops or shifting to less demanding alternatives.

Consumers have felt the brunt of this crisis through skyrocketing food prices. Low-income households, which spend a significant portion of their income on basic staples, are disproportionately affected. In regions like sub-Saharan Africa and parts of the Middle East, where food insecurity was already prevalent, rising costs have exacerbated hunger and malnutrition. Families face impossible choices between buying food, paying for fuel, or meeting other basic needs, deepening the human toll of the crisis.

The impact on global food systems has also raised fears of prolonged instability. As prices for essential commodities like wheat and corn remain volatile, importing nations face growing challenges in maintaining their food reserves and stabilizing domestic markets. This economic strain is particularly acute in emerging economies, which lack the financial resources to compete with wealthier nations for limited supplies.

A Call for Resilience and Diversification

The disruptions in grain and fertilizer supplies caused by the Russia-Ukraine war have underscored the fragility of global food systems. Over-reliance on a few key exporters for essential commodities has proven to be a significant vulnerability, leaving nations ill-prepared to handle the shocks of conflict and geopolitical upheaval.

The crisis serves as a stark reminder of the need for greater resilience and diversification. Strengthening local agricultural systems, investing in alternative supply chains, and fostering international cooperation are critical steps to mitigate future risks. As the world grapples with the long-term consequences of this disruption, it must prioritize strategies that ensure food security and economic stability in the face of global crises. This moment of upheaval offers an opportunity to reimagine and fortify the foundations of global agriculture, making them more robust and equitable for generations to come.

3.3 The Impact on Global Hunger and Agricultural Industries

The Russia-Ukraine war has intensified pre-existing vulnerabilities within global food systems, triggering a cascading crisis that affects millions worldwide. From escalating hunger among the most vulnerable to significant disruptions in agricultural industries, the consequences of this conflict extend far beyond the immediate regions involved. The situation underscores the urgent need for innovative, collaborative, and sustainable solutions to address these challenges.

Rising Hunger: Vulnerable Populations at Risk

The war has driven millions closer to the brink of hunger, worsening an already precarious global food security landscape. Prior to the conflict, Russia and Ukraine collectively accounted for a substantial share of global wheat, corn, and sunflower oil exports, serving as lifelines for many developing nations, particularly in Africa and the Middle East. Countries such as Yemen, Ethiopia, and Sudan, already facing food insecurity due to ongoing conflicts and climate challenges, have been hit hardest by the sudden halt in these critical supplies.

The United Nations World Food Programme (WFP), which relies heavily on Ukrainian grain for its operations, has reported severe difficulties in sourcing affordable food to meet growing demands. Rising costs and limited availability have reduced the WFP's capacity to deliver aid, leaving millions in desperate need. Families in affected regions are resorting to extreme coping mechanisms—reducing meal sizes, selling essential assets, and withdrawing children from school to cut expenses. These strategies, while offering temporary relief, perpetuate cycles of poverty and undermine the potential for long-term recovery and development.

Challenges for Developing Nations: Deepening Food Insecurity

Developing nations that rely heavily on food imports face a compounded crisis. Not only have global food prices surged due to the disruption of exports, but the scarcity of critical staples has strained both national budgets and household incomes. Countries already grappling with economic instability, debt burdens, and climate-related challenges have seen their food insecurity intensify, pushing millions into malnutrition and chronic hunger.

The repercussions are severe and multifaceted. Governments in food-importing nations are struggling to manage public discontent, as rising food prices spark protests and social unrest. Political instability, combined with economic hardship, creates volatile conditions that threaten regional peace and development. The inability to address these crises promptly risks reversing decades of progress in poverty reduction, education, and healthcare.

Strains on Global Agriculture: A Call for Innovation and Resilience

The war has exposed critical vulnerabilities in global agriculture, emphasizing the need for more robust and adaptive systems capable of withstanding future shocks. Farmers across the globe have felt the impact of skyrocketing prices for fertilizers, fuel, and other essential inputs, which have significantly increased production costs. While developed nations are able to absorb some of these costs through subsidies or pass them on to consumers, farmers in developing countries face harsher realities. Limited access to affordable fertilizers and modern farming technologies has led to declining yields, further deepening global food shortages.

Agricultural industries, already grappling with the impacts of climate change, are now struggling to adapt to the combined pressures of conflict and economic instability. In regions where droughts, floods, and unpredictable weather patterns have become the norm, the additional burden of rising input costs threatens to collapse fragile farming systems.

The crisis has highlighted the urgent need for innovative solutions to enhance agricultural productivity and resilience. Technologies such as drought-resistant crops, precision agriculture, and sustainable farming practices offer potential pathways to mitigate future risks. However, their widespread adoption requires significant investment, research, and international cooperation.

A Collective Response to a Global Challenge

The strain on global hunger and agricultural industries caused by the Russia-Ukraine war is a stark reminder of the interconnectedness of food systems. What affects one region reverberates across the world, impacting nations with varying levels of resilience and resources. Addressing this crisis requires immediate, coordinated action from governments, international organizations, and the private sector.

Investments in agricultural innovation, equitable trade policies, and targeted aid programs are essential to stabilizing global food systems. Strengthening local agriculture through sustainable practices, enhancing access to modern technologies, and fostering collaboration between nations are critical steps in building a resilient future.

As the global community grapples with the far-reaching consequences of this conflict, it is clear that the road to recovery will require not only resources but also a shared commitment to creating a more equitable and sustainable food system. By leveraging innovation, cooperation, and a sense of shared responsibility, the world can turn this crisis into an opportunity to fortify food security and support the livelihoods of millions for generations to come.

3.4 Toward a Resilient Global Food System

The Russia-Ukraine war has laid bare the vulnerabilities of the global food system, revealing the fragility of supply chains and the disproportionate reliance on a few key producers for staple commodities. However, this crisis also offers a pivotal opportunity for transformative change. By embracing diversification, strengthening local agricultural systems, and fostering global collaboration, humanity can create a robust and equitable food system capable of withstanding future shocks and ensuring long-term food security.

Diversifying Supply Chains: Reducing Dependence on Single Sources

The heavy dependence on Ukraine and Russia for staples such as wheat, corn, and sunflower oil has proven to be a critical weakness in global food systems. When these supply lines were disrupted, the repercussions were felt worldwide, leading to price surges and shortages that impacted millions. This crisis underscores the urgent need to diversify supply chains to reduce the risks associated with over-reliance on a limited number of producers.

Nations must prioritize the development of alternative agricultural trade partnerships. Countries in Africa and South America, rich in arable land and agricultural potential, present untapped opportunities for diversifying global food production. Supporting these regions with investments in infrastructure, technology, and sustainable practices can help balance global supply chains while fostering economic growth.

Crop diversification is another essential strategy. Over-dependence on a few staples leaves food systems highly vulnerable to disruptions. Encouraging the cultivation of a wider variety of crops enhances food security by creating alternative sources of nutrition, improving soil health, and promoting biodiversity. Policymakers and agricultural stakeholders must work together to incentivize this shift, making diversified farming economically viable and environmentally sustainable.

Strengthening Local Agriculture: Solutions for Food Security

Building resilient local agricultural systems is a cornerstone of food security. For many nations, particularly those in the developing world, reducing reliance on imports by increasing domestic food production can provide a reliable buffer against global disruptions.

Investments in agricultural infrastructure are crucial. Improved roads, cold storage facilities, and irrigation systems ensure that locally grown food can reach markets efficiently and maintain its quality. Enhanced infrastructure also reduces post-harvest losses, a persistent challenge in many developing countries.

Providing farmers with access to modern tools and resources is equally important. High-quality seeds, affordable fertilizers, and advanced machinery can significantly boost productivity, enabling farmers to meet growing demand even under challenging conditions. Additionally, targeted training programs on sustainable and climate-resilient farming practices empower farmers to adapt to environmental changes and market shifts.

Urban farming and community-supported agriculture (CSA) programs offer innovative solutions for bridging the gap between producers and consumers. By growing food closer to where it is consumed, these initiatives reduce transportation costs, cut emissions, and increase food availability in urban areas. Such localized efforts complement broader agricultural reforms, creating a multi-layered approach to strengthening food systems.

Collaborative Global Efforts: Addressing Hunger and Building Resilience

Transforming the global food system requires coordinated action from governments, international organizations, private enterprises, and civil society. Collaboration is essential not only for addressing immediate crises but also for laying the foundation for a more sustainable and equitable future.

Emergency Relief and Food Aid: In the short term, global efforts must focus on providing food aid to regions suffering from acute hunger. Organizations such as the World Food Programme (WFP) and the Food and Agriculture Organization (FAO) require consistent funding, political support, and logistical coordination to deliver aid effectively. Humanitarian responses should prioritize the most vulnerable populations while minimizing disruptions to local food markets.

Research and Innovation: Long-term food security depends on advancements in agricultural research. Developing climate-resilient crops, improving water management techniques, and innovating food storage and distribution technologies are critical to enhancing global agricultural productivity. Sharing these innovations across borders ensures that countries, particularly those with limited resources, can benefit from cutting-edge solutions.

Policy Alignment: Trade and agricultural policies must be aligned to promote stability and equity in global food markets. Removing barriers such as tariffs and export restrictions can prevent artificial shortages and price volatility. Multilateral agreements that encourage fair trade practices and prioritize food security over geopolitical interests are vital for stabilizing markets and fostering cooperation.

A Vision for a Resilient Future

The interconnected challenges of hunger, conflict, and climate change demand a comprehensive and unified response. The lessons from the Russia-Ukraine war serve as a stark reminder of the fragility of our global food systems but also highlight the opportunities for meaningful reform. By diversifying supply chains, strengthening local agriculture, and fostering global collaboration, humanity can build a food system that is equitable, sustainable, and resilient.

This vision requires not only resources and innovation but also a shared commitment to addressing hunger and inequality. Through collective action, the global community can ensure that future generations inherit a world where food is abundant, accessible, and secure for all.

Chapter 4: Trade and Supply Chain Chaos

The Russia-Ukraine war unleashed a cascade of disruptions across global trade and supply chains, exposing vulnerabilities in systems long assumed to be robust. What began as localized blockades and sanctions rapidly spiraled into a worldwide economic shockwave, with industries from agriculture to high-tech manufacturing feeling the strain. Ports once bustling with exports now lie silent, while sanctions against Russia have forced companies to rethink their reliance on traditional trade routes and partners. This chapter delves into the intricate web of global commerce, exploring how the war has reshaped trade dynamics, impacted key industries, and compelled nations to recalibrate their economic partnerships for a more uncertain world.

4.1 Blockades and Sanctions: Reshaping Global Trade

The Russia-Ukraine war has acted as a seismic force in global trade, disrupting established patterns and exposing the vulnerabilities of an interconnected economy. Blockades and sanctions—modern tools of economic warfare—have not only targeted the belligerent nations but have also caused widespread disruptions across international supply chains, redrawing the map of global commerce. This crisis has forced countries and businesses to rethink their trade strategies and partnerships, emphasizing the fragility and interconnectedness of global markets.

The Role of Blockades in Disrupting Critical Exports

Ukraine, often referred to as the "breadbasket of Europe," has historically been a vital player in the global trade of grains, oilseeds, and industrial metals. The onset of war turned its once-thriving Black Sea ports, such as Odessa and Mariupol, into contested zones. Blockades effectively cut off these critical export routes, leaving millions of tons of goods stranded. Ships that once carried wheat, sunflower oil, and steel to international markets were immobilized, creating severe bottlenecks and sending shockwaves across global supply chains.

The consequences of these blockades extended far beyond Ukraine. Nations reliant on Ukrainian exports, particularly in Africa, the Middle East, and parts of Asia, faced acute shortages of essential commodities. Grain prices surged, exacerbating food insecurity in regions already vulnerable to hunger. Oilseed shortages disrupted industries producing cooking oil and livestock feed, while the absence of Ukrainian steel affected construction and manufacturing sectors worldwide.

Efforts to mitigate these disruptions through alternative transport routes, such as railways connecting Ukraine to neighboring countries like Poland and Romania, proved insufficient. These overland routes lacked the capacity to handle the sheer volume of goods that typically flowed through Ukraine's ports. The logistical complexities of navigating war-torn regions further delayed shipments, increased transportation costs, and contributed to a global imbalance in supply and demand.

The blockades underscored the risks of over-reliance on single sources for critical commodities. They also highlighted the need for more resilient and diversified trade routes, capable of withstanding geopolitical disruptions.

Economic Warfare: The Global Impact of Sanctions on Russia

The sanctions imposed on Russia by Western nations in response to its invasion of Ukraine represent one of the most comprehensive economic campaigns in modern history. These measures targeted key sectors, including energy, finance, and technology, with the intent of undermining Russia's economic stability and limiting its capacity to sustain the war. However, the ripple effects of these sanctions extended far beyond Russia's borders, reshaping global trade and creating significant challenges for the international community.

Russia, as one of the world's largest exporters of oil, gas, and essential raw materials like aluminum, nickel, and fertilizers, played a central role in global supply chains. The sanctions disrupted these flows, causing price volatility and shortages in multiple sectors. European nations, heavily dependent on Russian energy, faced soaring costs and had to rapidly secure alternative suppliers. Emerging economies, less equipped to compete for these scarce resources, bore the brunt of rising prices and reduced access.

Financial sanctions added another layer of complexity, as restrictions on Russian banks and payment systems made international transactions with Russian entities increasingly difficult. Companies operating in Russia or relying on its exports were forced to navigate a labyrinth of legal and logistical hurdles. The exclusion of Russia from global trade agreements further complicated supply chains, forcing businesses to reroute goods and find new partners.

While the sanctions inflicted significant economic pain on Russia, they also triggered debates about their unintended consequences. Critics pointed out that the measures contributed to global inflation, strained energy markets, and deepened food insecurity in vulnerable regions. Proponents, however, argued that the sanctions were a necessary tool to apply economic pressure and isolate Russia diplomatically.

Trade Routes in Flux: A New Map for Global Commerce

The war has catalyzed a transformation in global trade routes and partnerships, as nations adapt to the disruptions caused by blockades and sanctions. Traditional corridors through Eastern Europe and Central Asia have been destabilized, prompting the exploration of alternative pathways and alliances.

One notable development is the increased attention on the Arctic route, which connects Europe and Asia via the Arctic Ocean. Once considered a marginal option, this route is gaining traction as melting ice makes it more navigable. While still fraught with environmental and logistical challenges, the Arctic route represents a potential alternative to disrupted traditional trade corridors.

China has emerged as a key player in this evolving landscape. As Russia pivots eastward to counteract its exclusion from Western markets, China has strengthened its economic ties with Moscow, securing discounted energy supplies and raw materials. This growing alignment highlights the formation of new economic blocs and raises concerns about a fragmented global trade system.

At the same time, Western nations have intensified efforts to establish trade agreements with emerging markets in Southeast Asia, South Asia, and Africa. These partnerships aim to reduce dependence on adversarial nations and create more resilient supply chains. India, for instance, has become a focal point for trade diversification, offering both a growing market and a strategic location for global commerce.

The trend of "friendshoring"—prioritizing trade partnerships with politically aligned nations—reflects a shift away from purely cost-driven trade policies. Regionalism is gaining prominence as countries seek to secure their economic interests while minimizing geopolitical risks.

Lessons for the Future

The disruptions to global trade caused by blockades and sanctions during the Russia-Ukraine war have underscored the fragility of current systems and the need for more adaptive strategies. Diversification of trade routes and partnerships, investment in resilient infrastructure, and a greater emphasis on regional collaboration are essential for mitigating future risks.

While the immediate impact of the war has been destabilizing, it has also prompted nations and businesses to rethink their approaches to global commerce. The lessons learned from this crisis will likely shape trade policies for years to come, fostering a more dynamic and interconnected world that is better equipped to navigate the uncertainties of an increasingly complex geopolitical landscape.

4.2 Industries Most Affected by Disrupted Supply Chains

The Russia-Ukraine war has laid bare the fragility of global supply chains, disrupting industries across the board and exposing the vulnerabilities of globalization. Blockades, sanctions, and geopolitical tensions have caused widespread production delays, skyrocketing costs, and significant shifts in consumer dynamics. The ripple effects of these disruptions have been particularly acute in three key sectors: manufacturing, food and agriculture, and energy.

Manufacturing Slowdowns: From Automobiles to Electronics

Manufacturing, the backbone of industrial economies, has been severely impacted by the war's disruption of critical supply chains. The automobile industry, already grappling with post-pandemic challenges, has faced severe shortages of essential raw materials. Ukraine and Russia, major suppliers of key components like palladium (used in catalytic converters) and neon gas (crucial for semiconductor production), saw their exports plummet due to conflict and sanctions. These shortages have caused widespread production delays, increased costs, and left assembly lines idle in many parts of the world.

For the electronics sector, the challenges have been equally daunting. Ukraine, a dominant supplier of high-purity neon gas used in chip manufacturing, experienced sharp declines in exports, further straining the already overburdened semiconductor industry. Smartphone and computer manufacturers were forced to delay product launches, raise prices, and reevaluate their supply chain strategies. The shortage of semiconductors, which began during the COVID-19 pandemic, has been exacerbated by the war, exposing the vulnerabilities of just-in-time manufacturing practices that rely on uninterrupted supply flows.

These disruptions have highlighted the need for greater supply chain diversification. Companies are now exploring alternative sources for critical materials, investing in local production capabilities, and rethinking their reliance on a handful of global suppliers.

Food and Agriculture: Supply Chain Breakdowns in Critical Commodities

The global food and agriculture sector has been deeply affected by the war, given Ukraine's critical role as a major exporter of grains, oilseeds, and fertilizers. Blockades in the Black Sea have choked off the flow of wheat, corn, and sunflower oil, leaving import-dependent nations scrambling to secure alternative supplies. This disruption has caused sharp price increases for basic staples, intensifying food insecurity in vulnerable regions across Africa, the Middle East, and Asia.

Fertilizer shortages have compounded the crisis. Russia, a leading exporter of nitrogen-based fertilizers and essential inputs like ammonia and potash, faced stringent sanctions, while Ukrainian fertilizer production was severely curtailed by the conflict. Farmers worldwide, particularly in developing nations, have struggled to afford these crucial inputs, leading to lower crop yields and pushing millions closer to hunger and poverty. The strain on global agriculture has been profound, with cascading effects on food production, availability, and affordability.

The food processing and distribution industries, heavily reliant on stable agricultural inputs, have also felt the impact. Rising costs for raw materials have led to higher consumer prices, forcing companies to pass these increases onto already stretched households. In some regions, food companies have had to scale back operations, further reducing access to critical supplies.

Energy Markets in Crisis: Ripple Effects on Transportation and Industry

The energy sector, deeply entangled in the geopolitical dynamics of the war, has experienced cascading effects across industries reliant on fuel and power. Europe's scramble to replace Russian natural gas triggered a surge in energy prices, which rippled through transportation networks and industrial operations worldwide. Logistics costs soared as fuel prices climbed, driving up the expense of shipping goods across borders and exacerbating delays in already strained supply chains.

Energy-intensive industries, such as steel, cement, and chemicals, were hit particularly hard. Rising input costs forced many factories in Europe to reduce production or temporarily shut down, leading to layoffs and disruptions across the value chain. The transportation sector, including aviation, shipping, and trucking, also struggled to absorb soaring fuel prices, resulting in higher freight charges and more expensive goods for consumers.

The knock-on effects extended to smaller businesses that depend on affordable energy to operate. SMEs, already weakened by the economic fallout of the pandemic, faced existential threats as energy bills rose beyond manageable levels. These cascading disruptions underscored the interconnectedness of the energy sector with virtually every other industry, highlighting the far-reaching consequences of supply chain instability.

A Web of Interconnected Crises

The disruptions caused by the Russia-Ukraine war illustrate how deeply interconnected global industries have become. Manufacturing, agriculture, and energy are not isolated sectors—they are part of a complex, interdependent network where the failure of one link reverberates throughout the system. The ripple effects of supply chain disruptions have underscored the urgent need for diversification, resilience, and innovation.

Governments and businesses are beginning to recognize the importance of investing in localized production, alternative trade routes, and sustainable practices. The lessons learned from this crisis are driving efforts to build more robust and adaptable supply chains, capable of weathering the uncertainties of a volatile geopolitical landscape. By addressing these vulnerabilities, the global economy can better prepare for future disruptions, ensuring stability and growth in an increasingly unpredictable world.

4.3 The Recalibration of Trade Partnerships

The Russia-Ukraine war has brought into sharp focus the vulnerabilities of global trade networks, forcing nations and industries to reevaluate their economic strategies. The disruption of traditional supply chains and the heightened geopolitical tensions have triggered a recalibration of trade partnerships, fostering the emergence of new alliances and shifting priorities toward resilience, trust, and regional integration. This evolving trade landscape underscores a pragmatic approach to mitigating risks and addressing the lessons of recent disruptions.

Shifting Alliances: The Emergence of New Trade Blocs

As the war disrupted established trade routes and sanctions isolated major players like Russia, the global trade map began to redraw itself around emerging alliances. Nations sought strategic partnerships grounded in shared interests, geographical advantages, and mutual resource dependencies.

China, for instance, strengthened its economic ties with Russia, leveraging discounted energy imports and expanding its influence in a world increasingly divided along geopolitical lines. This alignment not only provided Russia with an alternative to Western markets but also reinforced China's role as a pivotal player in reshaping global trade dynamics. Similarly, India adopted a pragmatic approach, maintaining its strong connections with Western economies while significantly increasing energy imports from Russia, capitalizing on favorable terms.

Beyond these prominent players, the Global South has emerged as a key actor in reshaping trade relationships. Developing nations in Africa, Asia, and Latin America have leveraged the global disruption to enhance South-South cooperation, reducing dependence on traditional Western markets. This trend is creating opportunities for more balanced trade dynamics, enabling these regions to assert greater autonomy in their economic strategies.

Friendshoring and Nearshoring: Reducing Dependence on Geopolitical Adversaries

The conflict has accelerated the adoption of friendshoring, a strategy in which governments and businesses prioritize sourcing and production within allied nations that share common values and geopolitical interests. By cultivating partnerships with trusted allies, countries aim to insulate their supply chains from disruptions caused by adversarial nations or unstable regions. Europe's pivot toward energy imports from reliable suppliers like Norway, the United States, and North Africa exemplifies this shift, as it seeks to replace Russian gas with more secure alternatives.

Nearshoring has gained similar traction, particularly among multinational corporations. Relocating production closer to home or to politically stable neighboring regions reduces transportation costs, mitigates supply chain risks, and enhances predictability in the flow of goods. For example, Mexico has become an increasingly attractive nearshoring destination for U.S. companies due to its proximity, cost advantages, and integration within the USMCA (United States-Mexico-Canada Agreement). This trend is reshaping manufacturing landscapes across North America, Europe, and parts of Asia.

The Rise of Regional Trade Agreements: A Response to Global Instability

Regional trade agreements have emerged as critical mechanisms for countering the uncertainties of global markets. By fostering economic cooperation and reducing barriers within specific regions, these agreements aim to create self-reliant markets that are less susceptible to external shocks.

The Comprehensive and Progressive Agreement for Trans-Pacific Partnership (CPTPP) has taken on renewed importance as member nations seek to strengthen economic ties and stabilize trade flows. In Europe, the war has intensified efforts to deepen integration within the European Union, particularly in energy, defense, and digital markets. ASEAN countries in Southeast Asia have similarly focused on bolstering intra-regional trade to cushion against volatility in global supply chains.

These regional frameworks serve not only as economic buffers but also as platforms for collective bargaining in an increasingly fragmented world. By uniting smaller economies within cohesive agreements, regions can amplify their influence on global trade policies and better navigate the complexities of shifting alliances.

Toward a Resilient Trade Landscape

The recalibration of trade partnerships marks a significant shift in how nations and industries approach global commerce. By fostering new alliances, prioritizing trusted partnerships, and embracing regional cooperation, the international community is laying the groundwork for a more resilient and adaptable trade system.

This transformation is not merely a reaction to current crises but a proactive step toward long-term sustainability and balance. Diversifying supply chains, strengthening local industries, and investing in regional frameworks will be crucial in navigating future challenges. While these changes are driven by necessity, they hold the promise of a more equitable and stable global economy, where collaboration and trust underpin the foundations of trade. In this evolving landscape, resilience is no longer an option—it is an imperative.

Chapter 5: Economic Fallout for Russia and Ukraine

The Russia-Ukraine war has left profound scars on the economies of both nations, reshaping their futures in ways few could have anticipated. For Ukraine, the destruction of infrastructure, loss of industries, and displacement of millions have created an economic crisis of unprecedented scale. The war has not only shattered homes and cities but also undermined the livelihoods and stability of an entire nation. On the other hand, Russia has faced the crippling effects of international sanctions, forcing its economy to recalibrate in the face of isolation. While both nations endure immense hardship, their responses to these challenges reveal stories of resilience, adaptation, and survival in the face of adversity. This chapter delves into the economic toll of the conflict, examining its immediate impact, long-term consequences, and the efforts to rebuild amid ongoing strife.

5.1 Ukraine's Devastated Economy: Destruction and Recovery Efforts

The Russia-Ukraine war has inflicted unparalleled devastation on Ukraine's economy, transforming a vibrant nation into a landscape of ruin and uncertainty. Once a key player in global agriculture, industry, and energy markets, Ukraine now faces an uphill battle to rebuild its economy while addressing the immense human and structural losses caused by the conflict. The impact has been felt across every sector, compounding the challenges of personal and national recovery for millions of Ukrainians.

The Toll of War: Infrastructure and Industrial Losses

The destruction of Ukraine's physical infrastructure has been one of the most visible consequences of the war, with wide-reaching implications for its economy.

Infrastructure in Ruins: The extensive damage to critical infrastructure—roads, bridges, railways, airports, and power grids—has paralyzed economic activity and disrupted logistics. Cities such as Mariupol, Kharkiv, and Kyiv have been heavily bombarded, leaving urban centers in ruins. Key transport hubs and energy facilities have been targeted, crippling the networks essential for trade and industrial production. Rebuilding this infrastructure will require years of effort and billions of dollars in investment.

Industrial Collapse: Ukraine's industrial heartland, particularly in the eastern regions, has been decimated. Factories, mines, and steel plants—once the backbone of the economy—have been either destroyed or rendered inoperable due to their location in active conflict zones. The steel industry, which accounted for a significant share of export revenues, has seen a dramatic decline, exacerbating economic instability.

Agricultural Disruptions: Known as the "breadbasket of Europe," Ukraine's agricultural sector has suffered devastating setbacks. Farmlands have been damaged by conflict, planting and harvesting disrupted, and export routes blocked. The loss of agricultural exports, including wheat, corn, and sunflower oil, has not only impacted global food security but also stripped Ukraine of a critical source of income.

The Human Cost: Unemployment and Population Displacement

The economic fallout from the war cannot be separated from its profound human consequences, as millions of Ukrainians face unemployment, displacement, and an uncertain future.

Widespread Unemployment: The closure of businesses and the destruction of industrial hubs have led to skyrocketing unemployment. Entire sectors, from manufacturing to services, have been crippled. Vulnerable groups, including women, children, and the elderly, face additional barriers to re-entering the workforce, exacerbating economic insecurity.

Mass Displacement: Over 14 million Ukrainians have been displaced, with millions seeking refuge abroad and others internally relocated. This mass exodus has strained local economies, disrupted communities, and created logistical challenges for both host countries and Ukraine itself.

Loss of Human Capital: The migration of skilled workers—including engineers, healthcare professionals, and educators—represents a significant loss for Ukraine's ability to rebuild. The departure of these critical talents has created a brain drain, complicating reconstruction efforts and reducing the availability of expertise needed to restore key industries.

Rebuilding Ukraine: International Aid and Domestic Strategies

Despite the immense challenges, efforts to rebuild Ukraine's economy are taking shape, supported by a combination of international assistance and domestic initiatives aimed at resilience and recovery.

International Aid: The global community has pledged billions of dollars to support Ukraine's recovery. Financial institutions such as the World Bank, International Monetary Fund (IMF), and European Union have provided grants and loans targeting infrastructure repair, economic stabilization, and humanitarian relief. NGOs and private donors are also contributing to rebuilding efforts, emphasizing the global solidarity behind Ukraine's recovery.

Focus on Infrastructure: Restoring key infrastructure—roads, bridges, railways, and power grids—is a top priority. International partnerships are aiding in the reconstruction of critical facilities, enabling transportation, trade, and energy production to resume. These efforts are essential for reviving economic activity and reconnecting Ukraine to global markets.

Stimulating Local Economies: Reviving small and medium-sized enterprises (SMEs) is central to Ukraine's recovery. Programs supporting agriculture, manufacturing, and entrepreneurship aim to create jobs and rebuild local economic resilience. Initiatives to modernize farming techniques and restore industrial production are particularly crucial for re-establishing Ukraine's economic identity.

Harnessing the Diaspora: Ukrainian professionals living abroad are being encouraged to contribute through remittances, investments, and technical expertise. Virtual collaboration platforms and returnee programs aim to reintegrate these skilled individuals into the rebuilding process, leveraging their knowledge and connections for national recovery.

A Testament to Resilience

The economic collapse brought on by the war has tested Ukraine's strength, but the determination to rebuild remains steadfast. The challenges are immense, from reconstructing infrastructure and industries to addressing the human toll of displacement and unemployment. Yet, these efforts represent more than a return to normalcy—they signify an opportunity to build a stronger, more resilient nation.

Ukraine's recovery is not just about restoring what was lost. It is a testament to the resilience of its people and the collective will to create a future that is more self-reliant, equitable, and prosperous. With the support of the international community and the resolve of its citizens, Ukraine stands poised to rise from the ashes, demonstrating the power of unity and perseverance in the face of adversity.

5.2 The Impact of Sanctions on Russia's Economy and Population

The sanctions imposed on Russia in response to its invasion of Ukraine represent one of the most extensive economic pressure campaigns in modern history. These measures were designed to isolate Russia from the global economy, targeting critical sectors like finance, trade, energy, and technology. The ripple effects have been severe, reshaping Russia's economic landscape while forcing its government and population to adapt to unprecedented challenges.

Sanctions in Action: Financial and Trade Restrictions

The sanctions have drastically disrupted Russia's financial and trade systems, cutting off critical lifelines and imposing significant economic strain.

Financial Isolation: The removal of key Russian banks from the SWIFT international payment system effectively severed their ability to conduct cross-border transactions. This restriction hindered international trade, complicated debt repayments, and limited access to foreign reserves. The result was a significant blow to Russia's ability to stabilize its currency and maintain import levels.

Frozen Assets: Hundreds of billions of dollars in Russia's foreign reserves were frozen in Western financial institutions. This deprived the Russian central bank of its capacity to manage currency volatility, causing the ruble to fluctuate wildly in the immediate aftermath of the sanctions.

Export Bans and Technology Restrictions: Critical exports to Russia, including semiconductors, advanced manufacturing equipment, and aerospace technologies, were banned. This stifled innovation and disrupted key sectors like defense, telecommunications, and manufacturing, leaving industries scrambling to find alternative suppliers or develop domestic capabilities.

Energy Markets Targeted: Russia's dominant position as an energy exporter was significantly undermined. Restrictions on oil and gas exports, including price caps and embargoes, slashed revenue streams. Europe's shift away from Russian energy added to the strain, forcing Russia to sell at discounted rates to new buyers, further diminishing profits.

Economic Strain on Households: Rising Prices and Declining Living Standards

Sanctions have not only targeted Russia's industries but also had profound effects on its citizens, who bear the brunt of rising costs, job losses, and reduced access to goods.

Inflation and Price Surges: Sanctions triggered sharp inflation, driving up the cost of basic goods such as food, medicine, and household items. Imported goods became prohibitively expensive or disappeared from shelves entirely as supply chains broke down. Everyday essentials saw price hikes, putting immense pressure on household budgets.

Job Losses and Wage Stagnation: Industries reliant on imported technologies and international markets, such as aviation and automotive manufacturing, faced significant layoffs. Wages stagnated even as the cost of living soared, eroding purchasing power and plunging many families into financial insecurity.

Diminished Quality of Life: For middle- and lower-income families, declining living standards became a harsh reality. Many were forced to cut back on healthcare, education, and even basic nutrition. The economic pressure created widespread frustration, with ripple effects on mental health and social stability.

Impact on Vulnerable Populations: Rural communities, pensioners, and low-income families have been hit hardest. These groups often lack access to alternative resources and rely heavily on subsidized services that have been scaled back. Inequalities have deepened, leaving many on the margins struggling to survive.

Coping Mechanisms: Russia's Shift Toward Economic Self-Sufficiency

In response to sanctions, Russia has adopted a series of strategies aimed at fostering self-reliance and mitigating economic damage. While these efforts have shown resilience in certain areas, they have also exposed the challenges of reversing decades of integration into the global economy.

Import Substitution Policies: Russia has prioritized domestic production to replace foreign goods, from consumer products to advanced technologies. These policies have yielded progress in agriculture and basic manufacturing but faced hurdles in high-tech industries where imported expertise and components are difficult to replace.

Strengthening Trade Partnerships: Cut off from traditional Western markets, Russia has turned to non-Western partners, including China, India, and nations in Africa and the Middle East. These partnerships have allowed some continuation of trade but often on less favorable terms, as new buyers exploit Russia's weakened negotiating position.

Energy Diversification: The loss of European markets has forced Russia to redirect energy exports to Asia, particularly China and India. Long-term agreements have provided a lifeline, but the discounts offered to attract these buyers have significantly reduced revenue. Infrastructure limitations, such as the need for new pipelines, have further complicated this shift.

Promoting Domestic Innovation: Sanctions have accelerated efforts to develop homegrown industries in sectors like agriculture, defense, and technology. While some success is evident in areas like food production, overcoming dependencies on imported machinery and expertise remains a formidable challenge.

A Reshaped Economic Landscape

The sanctions campaign has fundamentally altered Russia's economic trajectory. Industries have been forced to adapt, citizens are grappling with reduced living standards, and the government is navigating the complex realities of isolation from Western markets. While Russia has shown resilience in diversifying trade and fostering domestic production, these adaptations come with significant costs.

The long-term effectiveness of sanctions as a geopolitical tool remains a subject of debate. While they have undeniably strained Russia's economy and population, they have also highlighted the country's capacity to endure and innovate under pressure. This dual reality underscores the complexity of economic warfare in an interconnected world.

Ultimately, the sanctions have not only reshaped Russia's economy but also its place on the global stage, forcing a recalibration of policies, partnerships, and priorities in a rapidly changing environment.

5.3 The Resilience and Adaptation of Local Industries in Wartime

The Russia-Ukraine war has profoundly disrupted the economies of both nations, challenging local industries to adapt and innovate under extraordinary circumstances. Despite widespread destruction, economic isolation, and shifting trade dynamics, businesses in Ukraine and Russia have demonstrated remarkable resilience, ingenuity, and determination, finding ways to navigate an environment defined by uncertainty and crisis.

Ukraine's Wartime Economy: Innovating Amid Crisis

The war has tested Ukraine's economic foundations, compelling industries to pivot their focus and resources to meet the immediate needs of the nation. Despite these challenges, Ukrainian businesses have risen to the occasion, showcasing their capacity for rapid innovation and community-driven efforts.

Defense Manufacturing: In response to the pressing demands of war, Ukraine's industrial sector has reoriented itself toward defense production. From repurposing factories to manufacture drones and military equipment to small workshops producing munitions and protective gear, the defense sector has become a cornerstone of Ukraine's wartime economy. Collaboration between government, private manufacturers, and international allies has fueled these efforts.

Agricultural Adaptation: Known as the "breadbasket of Europe," Ukraine's agricultural sector has faced significant hurdles, including damaged farmland, disrupted supply chains, and blockaded ports. Nevertheless, farmers have employed innovative techniques such as precision agriculture and alternative transportation routes to continue exporting grains and oilseeds. These efforts, supported by international partnerships, have helped sustain Ukraine's role in global food systems.

Tech Sector Contributions: Ukraine's burgeoning tech industry has become a critical asset during the conflict. Tech companies have developed advanced cybersecurity solutions to protect critical infrastructure and communication tools to aid both military and civilian operations. This sector's ability to function remotely and innovate rapidly has underscored its resilience and importance in Ukraine's economy.

Grassroots Manufacturing and Community Support: Across the nation, small businesses and local communities have stepped up to fill critical gaps. From producing emergency medical supplies to providing essential consumer goods, these efforts reflect the resilience and solidarity of Ukrainian society. Community-driven initiatives, such as cooperative manufacturing, highlight the power of collective action in sustaining the economy during wartime.

Russia's Pivot: Domestic Production and Alternative Trade Partners

For Russia, the imposition of severe sanctions and its subsequent economic isolation have necessitated a complete reorientation of trade and industrial strategies. Russian industries have responded by focusing on domestic production and seeking alternative trade partnerships.

Import Substitution Strategies: Sanctions have restricted Russia's access to Western goods, spurring a push for domestic alternatives. Efforts to replace imported agricultural products, pharmaceuticals, and consumer goods have seen mixed success, but they have driven growth in local manufacturing and supply chains.

Energy Sector Adjustments: The energy sector, a cornerstone of Russia's economy, has adapted by redirecting oil and gas exports to non-Western markets, particularly China and India. Investments in refining and transportation infrastructure have been accelerated to support these new trade routes. Although the shift has been economically viable, it has often come at reduced profits and increased logistical costs.

New Trade Alliances: Russia has strengthened economic ties with nations in Asia, Africa, and the Middle East. These partnerships have enabled the continued exchange of goods, although at a smaller scale and less favorable terms than those previously enjoyed with Western markets. This recalibration has been crucial in maintaining economic stability despite isolation.

Localized Innovation: Russian businesses, particularly in technology and consumer goods, have turned to innovation to address gaps left by the exodus of multinational corporations. Startups and SMEs have developed domestic solutions to meet demand, from new software platforms to locally produced consumer electronics.

The Role of SMEs: Driving Local Recovery and Resilience

Small and medium-sized enterprises (SMEs) have emerged as critical drivers of resilience and adaptability in both Ukraine and Russia, acting as lifelines for local economies.

In Ukraine: SMEs have shifted their focus to produce goods essential for wartime survival, such as food, clothing, and emergency supplies. Many have also provided employment opportunities for displaced individuals, stabilizing communities and contributing to social cohesion. Programs supporting SMEs have become vital in fostering local economic recovery amid destruction.

In Russia: SMEs have shown remarkable agility in navigating sanctions and supply chain disruptions. Businesses have turned to local materials, expanded e-commerce operations, and explored niche markets to sustain their operations. By filling gaps left by international companies, SMEs have mitigated some of the economic fallout and provided jobs in affected regions.

Acts of Defiance and Hope

The resilience of local industries in Ukraine and Russia is more than a response to economic necessity—it is a powerful act of defiance and hope. In Ukraine, businesses have become integral to the nation's survival and recovery efforts, demonstrating an unyielding determination to rebuild in the face of adversity. In Russia, industries have adapted to an isolated and constrained environment, reflecting a pragmatic approach to enduring sanctions and maintaining domestic stability.

While the challenges faced by both nations are immense, the innovation and adaptability displayed by their industries underscore the potential for recovery and renewal. These efforts are laying the groundwork for future economic resilience, ensuring that even amid the turmoil of war, the seeds of progress and restoration are sown.

Chapter 6: Global Markets in Turmoil

The Russia-Ukraine war unleashed a cascade of economic disruptions that reverberated across the globe, shaking the foundations of markets already strained by the aftermath of a global pandemic. The conflict triggered surging inflation, heightened fears of recession, and sent financial markets into a state of heightened volatility. Emerging economies, grappling with rising debt and currency instability, found themselves on the brink of crisis, while multinational corporations scrambled to navigate fractured supply chains and shifting trade dynamics. As central banks and governments struggled to respond, the fragility of interconnected global markets became starkly evident, underscoring the urgent need for systemic reforms to bolster resilience. This chapter delves into the multifaceted impacts of the war on global markets, exploring the challenges faced and the lessons learned in an era of unprecedented economic turbulence.

Introduction: The Ripple Effects of a Global Shock

When the first shots of the Russia-Ukraine war echoed across Eastern Europe, the economic consequences reverberated far beyond the battlefield. What initially seemed like a regional conflict quickly morphed into a global crisis, destabilizing interconnected markets and laying bare the vulnerabilities of the globalized economy. Supply chains ground to a halt, energy and food prices surged to unprecedented levels, and financial markets, still fragile from the aftershocks of the COVID-19 pandemic, entered a new phase of volatility. The war underscored how deeply entwined the world's economies had become, turning local disruptions into worldwide ripple effects.

The fallout was immediate and multifaceted. Inflation soared as skyrocketing energy and commodity prices filtered through to every corner of the global economy. Central banks found themselves in a precarious position, balancing the need to combat inflation with fears of triggering recessions. Governments scrambled to deploy subsidies, stimulus packages, and emergency policies to shield their populations from escalating costs, while protests over rising living expenses erupted in several nations. Emerging economies, reliant on affordable imports and access to foreign capital, were among the hardest hit, teetering on the brink of financial crises as the war disrupted trade flows and drove up borrowing costs.

Corporations faced an equally tumultuous environment. Multinational firms had to navigate a maze of new trade barriers, sanctions, and logistical challenges, forcing them to rethink supply chain strategies and reassess market dependencies. Companies operating in energy-intensive sectors or reliant on raw materials from Ukraine and Russia bore the brunt of the disruption. At the same time, businesses in nonaligned or emerging markets found themselves caught between competing geopolitical pressures, further complicating operations.

The destabilization of global markets highlighted the fragility of systems once celebrated for their efficiency. Energy dependencies on a handful of suppliers, the just-in-time manufacturing model, and concentrated trade routes all proved ill-equipped to handle the strain of a large-scale conflict. The resulting crises in food security, energy availability, and financial stability prompted a global reckoning, with calls for diversification, resilience, and systemic reform growing louder.

This introduction delves into the initial economic shockwaves unleashed by the Russia-Ukraine war. From inflationary pressures to currency fluctuations and supply chain breakdowns, it sets the stage for a deeper exploration of how these disruptions have reshaped economies, industries, and global trade. The war is more than a geopolitical crisis; it is a defining moment for the modern economic order, revealing vulnerabilities that demand urgent attention and offering lessons that could reshape the future of global markets.

6.1 Inflation and Recession Fears

The Russia-Ukraine war unleashed a cascade of economic turmoil, sparking inflation and recession fears on a global scale. The conflict's immediate disruption to supply chains, energy markets, and commodity flows exacerbated preexisting vulnerabilities in a world still recovering from the COVID-19 pandemic. As inflation surged to levels unseen in decades, central banks struggled to find a balance between controlling skyrocketing prices and sustaining economic growth. Meanwhile, the specter of stagnation loomed, threatening to derail the fragile recovery of both developed and emerging economies.

Surging Commodity Prices: A Catalyst for Global Inflation

The war's most immediate and visible economic impact was the unprecedented surge in commodity prices. Both Russia and Ukraine are critical exporters of essential goods, and the disruption of their output reverberated through global markets.

Energy Prices

The war upended global energy markets, with Russian oil and gas exports severely curtailed due to sanctions and logistical barriers. Europe, heavily reliant on Russian gas, faced unprecedented utility costs, straining households and industries alike. The price of crude oil soared above $100 per barrel, driving up transportation and production costs worldwide. Energy-dependent industries such as transportation, chemicals, and manufacturing bore the brunt, passing on higher costs to consumers.

Food Prices

Ukraine's pivotal role in global grain and fertilizer markets made its inability to export a key driver of food inflation. Blockades in the Black Sea and damaged supply chains left millions of tons of wheat and corn stranded, sending global food prices spiraling upward. Vulnerable populations in developing nations felt the sharpest impact, as staples like bread and cooking oil became prohibitively expensive, exacerbating existing hunger crises.

Industrial Commodities

The war also disrupted supplies of critical metals like aluminum, nickel, and palladium, essential for automotive, electronics, and renewable energy sectors. The resulting shortages increased manufacturing costs, further fueling inflation in consumer goods and stalling progress in key industries such as electric vehicle production.

Central Bank Responses: Balancing Growth and Stability

In response to escalating inflation, central banks across the globe took decisive, albeit risky, action. The rapid implementation of tighter monetary policies highlighted the delicate balancing act required to stabilize economies without stifling growth.

Tightening Monetary Policies

Central banks, including the U.S. Federal Reserve and the European Central Bank, aggressively raised interest rates to temper inflation. While these measures succeeded in curbing demand to some extent, they also increased borrowing costs for businesses and individuals. This dampened investment, slowed consumer spending, and posed a significant risk to economic growth.

Currency Volatility

Interest rate hikes in advanced economies strengthened currencies like the U.S. dollar, creating a ripple effect in emerging markets. Many of these nations, with dollar-denominated debts, faced higher repayment costs as their local currencies depreciated. This currency instability amplified inflationary pressures in import-reliant economies, deepening financial vulnerabilities.

Stagnation Risks: The Looming Threat of Global Recession

The simultaneous pressures of rising prices and restrictive monetary policies gave rise to fears of stagflation—an economic condition characterized by stagnant growth and persistent inflation.

Slowing Growth

As businesses grappled with rising input costs and declining consumer demand, production slowed across key sectors. Manufacturing hubs in Europe, Asia, and the Americas faced significant slowdowns, particularly in energy-intensive industries like steel, automotive, and construction. Job cuts and reduced investments further compounded the economic malaise.

Global Recession Warnings

International organizations like the World Bank and the International Monetary Fund (IMF) issued warnings of a potential global recession. Export-dependent nations saw revenues plummet, while import-heavy economies struggled to manage surging costs. The cumulative effect was a contraction in economic activity across multiple regions, raising the prospect of a synchronized global downturn.

Widening Economic Inequality

Inflation disproportionately affected low-income households, whose budgets are heavily skewed toward necessities like food and energy. Rising costs eroded purchasing power, forcing many to make painful sacrifices, such as cutting back on meals, healthcare, and education. The unequal burden of inflation exacerbated existing inequalities, pushing millions into poverty and deepening social divides.

A Wake-Up Call for Resilient Economic Systems

The Russia-Ukraine war underscored the fragility of global economic systems and the urgent need for structural reform. The cascading inflationary pressures and recession fears revealed the vulnerabilities inherent in overly concentrated supply chains, energy dependencies, and financial systems. Policymakers were reminded of the importance of:

Diversification: Reducing reliance on single sources for energy, food, and raw materials to minimize future disruptions.

Resilience: Strengthening domestic supply chains and investing in renewable energy to insulate economies from external shocks.

Global Cooperation: Addressing cross-border challenges like inflation and recession requires collaborative solutions, from coordinated monetary policies to international trade reforms.

The economic upheaval caused by the war served as both a warning and an opportunity—highlighting the interconnected nature of modern economies while presenting a chance to build systems that are more adaptive, equitable, and sustainable in the face of future crises.

6.2 Financial Market Volatility

The Russia-Ukraine war introduced unprecedented volatility to global financial markets, rattling investor confidence, destabilizing currencies, and shifting preferences toward perceived safe-haven assets. The conflict's far-reaching impact was felt across stock exchanges, currency markets, and investment portfolios, forcing economies and investors to navigate an increasingly uncertain landscape.

Stock Markets in Flux: The Impact on Investor Confidence

Global stock markets reacted sharply to the outbreak of the conflict, with geopolitical uncertainty amplifying preexisting vulnerabilities in a world still recovering from the COVID-19 pandemic. Investor sentiment swung wildly as markets tried to absorb the immediate and long-term implications of the war.

Initial Sell-Offs: In the early days of the conflict, stock markets experienced a dramatic sell-off as investors fled riskier assets. Key indices like the S&P 500, FTSE 100, and Nikkei 225 posted steep declines, reflecting widespread concerns about disrupted supply chains, surging energy costs, and the potential economic fallout of sweeping sanctions on Russia. Emerging markets were particularly hard-hit, as capital outflows intensified amid rising global uncertainty.

Sectoral Winners and Losers: While broad indices suffered, specific sectors emerged as beneficiaries of the crisis. Energy and defense stocks saw a surge in investor interest, driven by Europe's urgent efforts to reduce reliance on Russian energy and increased global defense spending. Companies specializing in renewable energy technologies also attracted significant investment, as nations prioritized the transition to greener and more secure energy systems. Conversely, sectors like technology and manufacturing faced headwinds due to supply chain disruptions, rising raw material costs, and waning consumer demand.

Volatility Index Spike: The CBOE Volatility Index (VIX), often called the "fear gauge," surged to levels reminiscent of the early days of the pandemic, underscoring heightened market anxiety. This increase in volatility mirrored the uncertainty investors faced as they weighed geopolitical risks against economic fundamentals.

Currency Instability: Effects on Global Trade and Investment

The war triggered significant turbulence in currency markets, with sanctions, energy price spikes, and central bank actions creating an unpredictable environment for global trade and investment.

The Russian Ruble's Collapse and Recovery: The Russian ruble experienced a dramatic initial decline, plummeting to record lows following the imposition of sanctions that restricted Russia's access to foreign reserves and international payment systems. In response, the Russian government implemented stringent capital controls and pegged the ruble to commodities like gold and oil. These measures led to a surprising recovery, but the currency's stabilization came at the cost of reduced trade flexibility and heightened isolation from global markets.

The Strengthening U.S. Dollar: Amid the turmoil, the U.S. dollar strengthened significantly as investors sought safety in the world's reserve currency. While this bolstered the U.S. economy's global purchasing power, it posed challenges for emerging markets reliant on dollar-denominated debt. As local currencies weakened against the dollar, the cost of imports surged, exacerbating inflationary pressures and straining already fragile economies.

Eurozone Challenges: The euro depreciated as Europe faced dual crises of energy shortages and economic strain. Currency fluctuations further complicated trade within the Eurozone, adding to the financial burdens of exporters and importers navigating volatile commodity prices and disrupted supply chains.

Safe Havens: Gold and Other Assets in Turbulent Times

In periods of geopolitical and economic instability, investors traditionally turn to safe-haven assets to preserve wealth and hedge against uncertainty. The war reinforced this trend, with traditional and alternative assets experiencing varying levels of demand.

Gold's Resurgence: Gold prices soared during the conflict, reaffirming its status as a reliable store of value. As equity and currency markets wavered, investors flocked to the precious metal, which has historically served as a hedge against geopolitical risk and inflation. Central banks in some regions also increased their gold reserves as a buffer against potential currency devaluation.

Cryptocurrency's Ambiguous Role: Cryptocurrencies like Bitcoin initially gained traction in conflict zones as tools for cross-border transactions and financial sovereignty. However, their speculative nature, regulatory scrutiny, and susceptibility to market volatility limited their appeal as true safe-haven assets. While adoption grew in specific contexts, cryptocurrencies remained a niche option compared to traditional assets like gold and government bonds.

Government Bonds: Stable government securities, such as U.S. Treasury bonds and German bunds, attracted significant inflows as investors sought low-risk options. The increased demand for these bonds lowered yields, reflecting a flight to safety during the uncertainty of the war.

The financial market volatility spurred by the Russia-Ukraine war exposed the interconnectedness of global economies and their susceptibility to geopolitical disruptions. Investors faced a stark reminder of the importance of diversification, risk management, and adaptability in navigating unpredictable market conditions. The crisis underscored the need for robust strategies that balance short-term protective measures with long-term resilience, offering critical lessons for managing future economic shocks.

6.3 Impact on Emerging Economies and Global Debt Crises

The Russia-Ukraine war exacerbated economic challenges for emerging economies, amplifying vulnerabilities that had been building over years of global economic volatility. The conflict disrupted trade flows, destabilized currencies, and intensified inflationary pressures, leaving many developing nations struggling to maintain financial stability. While international financial institutions (IFIs) attempted to provide relief, their efforts often fell short of addressing the systemic challenges that these nations faced.

Currency Depreciation and Rising Import Costs

Emerging economies bore the brunt of the war's ripple effects on global markets, particularly in the form of currency depreciation and soaring import costs.

Weakened Currencies: As global investors sought refuge in safe-haven assets like the U.S. dollar, the currencies of emerging markets depreciated significantly. For countries reliant on imports of fuel, grain, and fertilizers, this devaluation magnified the cost of essential goods. Nations across Sub-Saharan Africa, South Asia, and Latin America faced sharp increases in import bills, creating fiscal imbalances and heightening economic distress.

Inflationary Pressures: Currency depreciation directly fueled inflation in countries heavily reliant on imported commodities. Food and energy prices soared, disproportionately affecting low-income households that spend the majority of their income on basic necessities. In countries like Ghana and Pakistan, these surges in living costs led to widespread public unrest and deepened existing socio-economic inequalities.

Trade Deficits: The combination of higher import costs and disrupted export markets widened trade deficits across many developing economies. For nations dependent on exports of raw materials or low-value goods, the economic imbalance reduced foreign currency reserves and constrained their ability to manage fiscal and monetary policy effectively.

Debt Burdens: Escalating Challenges for Developing Nations

The war compounded an already precarious global debt situation, pushing many emerging economies closer to financial crises.

Rising Borrowing Costs: As central banks in advanced economies raised interest rates to combat inflation, the cost of borrowing escalated for emerging markets. Countries like Sri Lanka and Zambia, already grappling with unsustainable debt levels, faced surging repayment obligations. Some nations defaulted on their debts, triggering a cascade of economic consequences, including reduced investor confidence and limited access to future credit.

Limited Fiscal Space: Governments in developing nations found themselves with little fiscal capacity to respond to the crisis. With public resources stretched thin to manage inflation and provide food subsidies, long-term investments in infrastructure, healthcare, and education were deprioritized. This lack of fiscal space constrained their ability to foster economic recovery and address social inequalities.

The Vicious Cycle of Instability: The convergence of rising debt, slowing economic growth, and depreciating currencies created a vicious cycle for many developing nations. With limited capacity to attract foreign investment or implement structural reforms, these countries became trapped in a loop of financial instability that perpetuated poverty and hindered development.

The Role of International Financial Institutions: Support and Gaps

International financial institutions played a critical role in mitigating the immediate impacts of the crisis but revealed significant shortcomings in addressing the broader structural challenges faced by emerging economies.

Emergency Financing: The IMF and World Bank mobilized funds through initiatives like the IMF's Rapid Credit Facility and World Bank's crisis response programs, offering liquidity and debt relief to vulnerable nations. While these efforts helped stabilize some economies in the short term, they often fell short of meeting the long-term needs of countries grappling with systemic challenges.

Policy Conditionality: Many developing nations criticized the stringent conditions tied to financial assistance, such as austerity measures, which disproportionately impacted vulnerable populations. These measures often required cuts to social services and public spending, exacerbating inequality and undermining public trust in governments and international institutions.

Gaps in Global Coordination: The fragmented international response to the crisis underscored the need for cohesive strategies to address interconnected issues like food security, energy access, and debt sustainability. Developing nations, particularly those outside high-priority geopolitical regions, were often left to navigate the crisis with insufficient support and resources.

The Russia-Ukraine war laid bare the fragility of emerging economies in the face of global disruptions. While international financial institutions provided critical relief, the crisis revealed deep gaps in the global financial architecture and underscored the urgent need for structural reforms. Moving forward, fostering resilience in developing economies will require innovative financing mechanisms, equitable international support, and greater collaboration among nations to address systemic vulnerabilities and prevent future crises. By addressing these challenges proactively, the global community can create a more stable and inclusive economic landscape.

6.4 Multinational Corporations Navigating Disruptions

The Russia-Ukraine war presented multinational corporations (MNCs) with unprecedented challenges, disrupting operations, destabilizing markets, and amplifying geopolitical risks. These obstacles forced companies to confront vulnerabilities in their business models while driving innovations and strategic shifts that will likely define the future of global commerce. From supply chain reconfigurations to long-term operational changes, MNCs had to adapt quickly to navigate this volatile landscape.

Supply Chain Reconfigurations: Coping with Uncertainty

The war severely disrupted global supply chains, pushing MNCs to reevaluate their logistics strategies and sourcing practices to maintain operational continuity.

Immediate Impacts: Critical supply routes through Eastern Europe were blocked, creating significant delays and escalating transportation costs. Industries reliant on raw materials from Ukraine and Russia—such as energy, agriculture, and metals—faced acute shortages. This disruption exposed the fragility of existing supply chains that depended heavily on a few high-risk regions.

Localized Manufacturing: In response, many corporations accelerated investments in localized manufacturing closer to their end markets. By producing goods within regional hubs, companies reduced their dependence on long-haul supply chains and high-risk regions. This shift not only mitigated logistical risks but also enabled quicker response times to market demands.

Inventory Management Shifts: The just-in-time inventory model, once celebrated for its efficiency, was challenged by the unpredictability caused by the conflict. Companies began shifting toward hybrid inventory models that included buffer stocks and a diversified supplier base. This approach provided greater flexibility and reduced the risk of supply shortages during crises.

Corporate Strategies: Diversifying Markets and Resources

To address the economic volatility and geopolitical risks posed by the war, MNCs adopted strategies to diversify their markets and resources.

Market Realignment: The imposition of sanctions on Russia forced many corporations to scale back or exit operations in the region. This prompted a redirection of investments toward emerging markets in Asia, Africa, and Latin America. These regions, with their growing consumer bases and developing economies, have become increasingly critical to global trade and corporate growth strategies.

Resource Diversification: Industries that relied on Russian energy and Ukrainian commodities had to quickly find alternative suppliers. Automotive manufacturers, for example, sought rare earth materials from new sources outside Russia, while agribusinesses expanded partnerships with grain producers in Latin America. This diversification reduced dependency on geopolitically unstable regions while ensuring continuity of supply.

Geopolitical Risk Management: The war underscored the need to incorporate geopolitical risks into corporate decision-making processes. Companies strengthened compliance systems to navigate sanctions and regulatory challenges effectively. Additionally, many implemented contingency plans and scenario analysis to better prepare for future disruptions.

The Reshaping of Global Business Models: Long-Term Implications

The lessons learned during this period of disruption have catalyzed lasting changes in how multinational corporations operate, pushing them toward more resilient and sustainable business models.

Digital Transformation: The adoption of digital tools and technologies accelerated as companies sought greater visibility and control over their operations. Predictive analytics, blockchain technology, and AI-powered supply chain monitoring systems became essential for identifying and addressing potential disruptions in real time. These tools improved decision-making and streamlined global logistics.

Sustainability and Resilience: The crisis reinforced the importance of sustainability as a core component of corporate strategy. Companies increasingly integrated renewable energy sources, energy-efficient technologies, and circular economy practices into their operations. By prioritizing sustainability, MNCs not only reduced their environmental impact but also built resilience against future economic and environmental shocks.

Collaborative Ecosystems: The complexity of global challenges necessitated collaboration across sectors. Partnerships between corporations, governments, and NGOs emerged as critical strategies for addressing shared issues, such as supply chain disruptions and energy shortages. Collaborative models, including shared logistics networks and joint investments in green technologies, demonstrated the potential for collective resilience.

The Russia-Ukraine war marked a pivotal moment for multinational corporations, exposing systemic vulnerabilities while spurring innovation and adaptation. The shift toward diversified supply chains, market realignment, and sustainable practices reflects a broader transformation in global business. As MNCs navigate the complexities of this new landscape, they are not only addressing immediate risks but also laying the groundwork for a more resilient, adaptable, and equitable global economy. These strategic changes, driven by necessity, will shape the future of multinational operations and global commerce for years to come.

6.5 Lessons for Future Resilience

The Russia-Ukraine war has been a pivotal moment for the global economy, highlighting both the vulnerabilities and the interconnectedness of international markets. The cascading disruptions in energy, trade, and financial systems exposed systemic weaknesses but also created a unique opportunity to build a more resilient, sustainable, and inclusive global economy. By addressing these weaknesses through strategic reforms, collaborative efforts, and forward-thinking investments, nations and businesses can better prepare for future crises.

Addressing Systemic Vulnerabilities in Global Markets

The war underscored critical weaknesses in the global economic infrastructure, prompting the need for comprehensive reforms.

Energy Dependencies: The conflict laid bare the dangers of over-reliance on singular energy sources, particularly Russian oil and gas. This dependency left nations vulnerable to price volatility and supply disruptions. A transition toward diversified and renewable energy sources is essential to reducing these risks. Governments and industries must accelerate investments in solar, wind, and other clean energy technologies to ensure energy security and sustainability.

Supply Chain Overhaul: Global supply chains, optimized for efficiency through just-in-time manufacturing, proved ill-equipped to handle sudden disruptions. Industries faced shortages and delays, exposing the need for more robust supply chain models. Companies should adopt strategies that include redundancy, nearshoring, and advanced digital tracking systems. These measures can create supply chains that are more flexible, localized, and resilient to geopolitical shocks.

Financial Market Stability: The sharp fluctuations in global stock markets and currency exchanges during the crisis revealed the fragility of financial systems in the face of geopolitical instability. Strengthened regulatory frameworks and cross-border financial safeguards are necessary to stabilize markets and prevent panic-induced economic instability. Mechanisms such as coordinated monetary policies and global financial stress tests can provide a buffer against future shocks.

The Case for Collaborative Solutions: Strengthening Multilateral Cooperation

The crisis reinforced the importance of global cooperation in managing economic disruptions and fostering stability.

International Agreements: Stronger international trade and energy agreements are crucial for mitigating the impact of future crises. Multilateral institutions like the World Trade Organization (WTO) and International Monetary Fund (IMF) can play pivotal roles in ensuring equitable resource distribution and fostering economic stability. These agreements must prioritize transparency, fairness, and the inclusion of emerging economies.

Regional Alliances: Regional trade blocs such as the European Union (EU) and ASEAN demonstrated their capacity to pool resources and implement coordinated strategies during the crisis. Expanding these alliances to include broader multilateral cooperation can amplify their effectiveness. For example, cross-regional partnerships that integrate trade, energy, and security policies can create a more resilient global economic framework.

Public-Private Partnerships: Collaboration between governments, corporations, and non-governmental organizations (NGOs) is essential for addressing global challenges. Joint initiatives such as infrastructure development, renewable energy projects, and shared technology investments can foster resilience and innovation. These partnerships enable the pooling of resources and expertise to tackle complex issues more effectively.

Investing in Sustainable and Inclusive Economic Growth

To ensure long-term resilience, the global economy must shift toward growth models that prioritize sustainability and inclusivity.

Green Economy Transition: The crisis highlighted the urgency of transitioning to a green economy. Investments in renewable energy, electric mobility, and circular economy practices can reduce dependence on volatile fossil fuel markets while addressing climate change. Governments and businesses must prioritize policies that incentivize clean energy adoption and support the development of sustainable industries.

Inclusive Economic Policies: The economic fallout of the war disproportionately affected vulnerable populations and emerging economies, exacerbating inequalities. Inclusive growth policies—such as accessible financing for small businesses, vocational training programs, and equitable wealth distribution—are essential for building economic stability. Targeted interventions can help marginalized communities and nations recover more quickly and sustainably.

Innovation as a Pillar of Growth: Investing in research and technology is critical for economic resilience and diversification. Emerging technologies such as artificial intelligence, blockchain, and advanced logistics can enhance efficiency and adaptability across industries. By fostering a culture of innovation, economies can better respond to changing circumstances and seize new opportunities.

A Path Forward

The Russia-Ukraine war has been a stark reminder of the interconnectedness and fragility of global markets. However, it also serves as a call to action. The international community must use this moment to address vulnerabilities and redefine resilience through collaborative, sustainable, and inclusive strategies. By learning from these disruptions and investing in long-term growth, nations and corporations can create a future where economies are not only prepared to withstand crises but also positioned to thrive in their aftermath. This transformative approach promises a world of greater stability, equity, and prosperity for generations to come.

Chapter 7: The Geopolitics of Sanctions

Sanctions have long been wielded as a powerful geopolitical tool, designed to coerce, deter, or punish nations that defy international norms. The Russia-Ukraine war has reignited debates about their effectiveness, fairness, and unintended consequences. As Western nations imposed sweeping sanctions on Russia, the global economy experienced profound ripple effects, reshaping alliances, disrupting trade, and exposing vulnerabilities in interconnected systems. This chapter delves into the multifaceted role of sanctions during the conflict, examining their intended goals, their impact on global power dynamics, and the lessons they offer for future policy-making. Through an exploration of their geopolitical significance, we aim to uncover the complexities of sanctions as instruments of influence in an increasingly multipolar world.

7.1 The Effectiveness of Sanctions

Sanctions, long employed as a tool of geopolitical strategy, are designed to exert economic and political pressure on nations to change their behavior without resorting to military conflict. The Russia-Ukraine war has placed sanctions at the forefront of international responses, with Western nations implementing an extensive and coordinated campaign to isolate Russia economically and politically. However, assessing the effectiveness of these measures reveals both their strengths and inherent limitations.

Measuring Success: Sanctions as Tools of Pressure

The primary objective of sanctions is to coerce a target nation into altering its behavior by imposing economic hardship on its government, critical industries, and influential individuals. In response to the Russia-Ukraine conflict, sanctions were implemented to achieve several specific goals:

Financial Disruption: Freezing Russian central bank reserves and excluding major banks from the SWIFT global payment system disrupted Russia's financial connectivity, making it harder to engage in international trade and manage currency stability.

Sectoral Targeting: Key sectors like energy, defense, and technology were undermined through export controls and import bans, limiting access to critical components, technology, and foreign markets.

Pressure on Elites: Sanctions on oligarchs and political elites included asset freezes, travel bans, and restrictions on luxury goods. These measures aimed to create internal pressure on the Russian leadership by targeting influential figures who benefit from the existing regime.

While these sanctions caused severe economic strain, their ability to achieve broader political objectives, such as ending the conflict or forcing policy changes, remains ambiguous. Economic destabilization alone does not guarantee a reversal of strategic goals, especially for nations like Russia, which appear willing to absorb long-term costs to achieve geopolitical ambitions.

Economic Isolation vs. Political Influence

Sanctions against Russia have effectively severed much of the country's access to global financial systems and markets. Removing Russian banks from SWIFT and freezing foreign reserves cut off critical lifelines for trade and currency stabilization. However, economic isolation does not always equate to political leverage.

Adaptation Through Alternative Alliances: Russia has shifted its trade focus to non-Western partners, including China, India, and Middle Eastern nations. This pivot has allowed Russia to sustain critical sectors, particularly energy, through bilateral trade agreements and discounted exports. While these deals come with compromises, they mitigate the full impact of sanctions.

Self-Sufficiency Efforts: The sanctions spurred domestic production in key sectors like technology and energy, reducing reliance on foreign imports. While these efforts often fall short of replacing high-quality international goods, they demonstrate the resilience of sanctioned nations in adapting to restrictions.

Political Entrenchment: Sanctions can harden political resolve rather than compel concessions. In Russia's case, the sanctions were framed domestically as Western aggression, bolstering nationalist sentiment and strengthening the government's narrative.

This dynamic highlights a core limitation of sanctions: while they can inflict significant economic pain, their success in achieving political influence depends on the target nation's capacity to adapt and its strategic priorities.

The Role of Multilateral Coordination in Sanctions Enforcement

The effectiveness of sanctions is amplified through multilateral cooperation, as unified action minimizes loopholes and increases pressure on the target. The response to the Russia-Ukraine war showcased unprecedented coordination among Western nations, including the European Union, the United States, Canada, Japan, and others.

Amplified Impact Through Unity: The collective imposition of sanctions closed many avenues for Russia to bypass restrictions. By targeting interconnected systems—financial networks, supply chains, and technology exports—this unity increased the severity of the sanctions' impact.

Challenges in Global Consensus: Not all nations aligned with the sanctions. Major economies like China and India maintained trade ties with Russia, purchasing discounted energy and commodities. Additionally, several developing nations chose neutrality, prioritizing their economic interests over geopolitical alignment. These gaps reduced the overall efficacy of the sanctions, underscoring the difficulty of achieving universal compliance.

Internal Tensions Among Allies: Differences in economic reliance on Russian energy and trade created friction within the Western bloc. For instance, European countries faced higher energy costs and supply challenges, complicating their ability to sustain long-term measures without domestic backlash.

Refining Sanctions as a Geopolitical Tool

The Russia-Ukraine conflict has provided valuable insights into the strengths and weaknesses of sanctions as an instrument of geopolitical strategy:

Targeted Approaches: Future sanctions must aim for greater precision, minimizing collateral damage to civilians and neutral third parties. Enhanced mechanisms for assessing and mitigating unintended consequences can improve their humanitarian outcomes.

Global Coordination: Efforts to expand multilateral participation in sanctions enforcement are essential. Engaging neutral or non-aligned nations through diplomatic channels can reduce opportunities for the target nation to bypass restrictions.

Balancing Economic and Political Objectives: Sanctions should be part of a broader strategy that includes diplomacy, economic incentives, and other tools to influence behavior. Economic pressure alone often falls short of achieving complex political goals.

In conclusion, sanctions are a potent yet imperfect tool of international diplomacy. While they can disrupt economies and signal international condemnation, their effectiveness hinges on the resilience of the target nation, the coherence of enforcement, and the broader geopolitical context. The Russia-Ukraine war has underscored both the potential and the limitations of sanctions, offering lessons for refining their application in future conflicts.

7.2 Unintended Consequences of Sanctions

Sanctions, often considered a non-violent method to exert pressure on nations, carry significant unintended consequences that extend far beyond their primary targets. While intended to influence political behavior or weaken a nation's economic base, sanctions frequently disrupt lives, destabilize economies, and strain international relations. The Russia-Ukraine war has highlighted these complexities, demonstrating that sanctions are not as precise a geopolitical tool as they are often assumed to be.

Collateral Damage: Impact on Civilians and Neutral Nations

One of the most immediate and visible consequences of sanctions is their effect on civilian populations, both within the targeted nation and in countries uninvolved in the conflict.

Within the Target Nation: In Russia, sanctions have led to widespread economic hardship, hitting civilians hardest. Job losses, skyrocketing inflation, and restricted access to essential goods, including medicines and food, have disproportionately affected middle- and lower-income families. Urban residents have experienced a decline in living standards, while rural areas, already economically fragile, have been further marginalized. This broad economic impact has widened social inequalities and deepened poverty.

In Neutral Nations: Sanctions often have a ripple effect, disrupting trade and economic stability in neutral countries. For instance:

✓ Nations reliant on Russian energy and agricultural exports, such as India, Turkey, and several African countries, have faced significant price increases and supply shortages.

✓ Developing economies dependent on imports of Russian fertilizer or Ukrainian grain have grappled with food insecurity, compounding pre-existing economic vulnerabilities.

✓ Neutral countries caught in the web of sanctions inadvertently suffer slowed economic growth as critical supply chains falter.

This collateral damage underscores the ethical and practical challenges of sanction policies, particularly when their effects exacerbate humanitarian crises in nations beyond the intended target.

Backfire Effects: Strengthening Resilience in Targeted Nations

Sanctions are designed to weaken a regime by creating public dissatisfaction and economic hardship. However, they often produce unintended backfire effects that consolidate power and bolster domestic resolve.

Nationalism and Solidarity: In Russia, sanctions have been framed as evidence of Western aggression, reinforcing nationalist narratives and fostering public support for the government. This "rally-around-the-flag" effect has united many citizens against perceived external threats, even when they experience economic hardship. Such dynamics can entrench political leadership, complicating efforts to drive change.

Economic Adaptation: Targeted nations often adapt to sanctions by fostering self-reliance and building alternative systems:

✓ Russia has expanded domestic production in key sectors like agriculture, technology, and manufacturing, reducing dependence on foreign imports.

✓ New trade partnerships with countries like China, India, and Turkey have allowed Russia to maintain critical exports, albeit at discounted prices and reduced profitability.

✓ Innovative financial mechanisms, such as alternative payment systems, have been developed to bypass restrictions, showcasing resilience in the face of economic isolation.

These unintended consequences highlight a key limitation of sanctions: they may weaken economies but often fail to dismantle the political or economic structures they target.

Disruption to Global Supply Chains and Markets

Sanctions against a major global economy like Russia inevitably have far-reaching effects on international trade and supply chains, often causing economic turbulence that transcends borders.

Energy Market Volatility: Restrictions on Russian oil and gas exports have destabilized global energy markets. Europe, heavily dependent on Russian energy before the war, faced soaring utility costs and supply shortages, prompting emergency measures and shifts toward alternative suppliers. However, this disruption rippled across global markets, driving up energy prices worldwide and exacerbating inflation in vulnerable economies.

Food and Agricultural Commodities: Sanctions on Russian fertilizers and disruptions to Ukrainian grain exports have intensified global food insecurity. Developing nations, particularly in Africa and the Middle East, have struggled with rising food costs and shortages, placing millions at risk of hunger. This dynamic has widened economic inequalities and fueled social unrest in affected regions.

Critical Industries: Sanctions targeting Russian exports of raw materials, such as palladium, nickel, and aluminum, have caused shortages in industries like automotive manufacturing, aerospace, and electronics. These disruptions have delayed production, increased costs, and driven inflation in consumer goods worldwide.

The interconnectedness of modern economies means that sanctions can unintentionally amplify global supply chain fragility, leaving neutral parties and allies grappling with unforeseen economic consequences.

Rethinking Sanction Strategies: Minimizing Unintended Consequences

The Russia-Ukraine conflict has underscored the complexities of using sanctions as a geopolitical instrument. To make sanctions more effective while minimizing their unintended consequences, policymakers must consider the following:

Targeted and Strategic Implementation: Narrowly tailored sanctions that focus on specific industries, individuals, or financial networks can limit collateral damage. For example, targeting military suppliers or oligarchs directly involved in political decision-making may yield greater impact than broad, sector-wide restrictions.

Global Coordination: Greater multilateral cooperation is essential to close loopholes and ensure enforcement. Engaging non-aligned nations and building consensus among allies can amplify the impact of sanctions while reducing the potential for circumvention.

Humanitarian Exemptions: Sanction regimes must include provisions to protect civilian populations. Allowing humanitarian aid, medicines, and essential goods to flow into targeted nations can prevent unnecessary suffering and mitigate backlash.

Long-Term Solutions: Investments in energy diversification, food security, and supply chain resilience can reduce reliance on vulnerable systems and mitigate the broader economic fallout of future sanctions.

In conclusion, sanctions remain a powerful yet imperfect tool for addressing geopolitical conflicts. While they can deliver significant economic blows to target nations, their unintended consequences—impacting civilians, neutral parties, and global markets—highlight the need for more strategic and humane approaches. The Russia-Ukraine conflict provides valuable lessons on balancing effectiveness with ethical considerations, emphasizing the importance of collaboration, precision, and resilience in shaping future sanction policies.

7.3 Realignment of Global Alliances

The sanctions imposed during the Russia-Ukraine conflict have triggered profound changes in the global geopolitical and economic order, forcing nations to reevaluate alliances and trade strategies. These measures, aimed at isolating Russia and influencing its behavior, have catalyzed shifts in partnerships, strengthened regional cooperation, and highlighted a growing divergence from traditional Western-dominated frameworks. The evolving dynamics underscore the interconnectedness of global trade and politics, revealing how sanctions can spur realignments that extend well beyond their immediate targets.

The Emergence of Alternative Economic Blocs

Sanctions have accelerated efforts by countries outside the Western sphere to establish alternative frameworks for trade, finance, and cooperation, reducing reliance on traditional global systems.

BRICS Expansion and De-Dollarization: The BRICS nations—Brazil, Russia, India, China, and South Africa—have intensified efforts to reduce dependency on U.S.-led financial systems. Proposals for a BRICS alternative to the SWIFT payment network and discussions around creating a common currency for trade have gained momentum. These moves reflect a broader shift toward de-dollarization, with member nations seeking to insulate their economies from Western sanctions and economic volatility.

Eurasian Economic Integration: Russia has sought to deepen economic ties within the Eurasian Economic Union (EAEU), fostering closer trade relations with member states such as Belarus, Armenia, Kazakhstan, and Kyrgyzstan. This regional bloc aims to create a collaborative economic framework that minimizes the impact of sanctions, emphasizing mutual trade agreements and shared infrastructure projects.

Middle Eastern and Asian Collaborations: Energy-rich nations in the Middle East, including Saudi Arabia and the UAE, have strengthened trade and energy partnerships with Russia, leveraging their resources to create mutually beneficial arrangements. Meanwhile, China's continued imports of Russian energy and commodities underscore its role as a pivotal partner in the emerging economic bloc, further solidifying its influence in the shifting global order.

Strengthened Ties Between Sanctioned Nations and Non-Western Powers

The imposition of sanctions has prompted targeted nations to forge closer relationships with non-Western powers, creating a network of alternative alliances driven by shared economic and geopolitical interests.

Russia and China: A Strategic Partnership: The Russia-China partnership has deepened, with China capitalizing on discounted Russian energy and raw materials. Both nations have collaborated on developing financial systems and technology infrastructure to counteract Western dominance. This partnership exemplifies the realignment of global power centers, with Beijing and Moscow working to create a parallel economic order.

Sanctioned States Supporting Each Other: Countries like Iran, North Korea, and Venezuela have aligned with Russia, sharing resources, expertise, and strategies to navigate economic isolation. These alliances, while complex and sometimes fraught with mistrust, underscore a growing trend of cooperation among nations outside Western influence.

Non-Aligned Pragmatism in the Global South: Many nations in Africa, Asia, and Latin America have adopted a pragmatic approach, maintaining trade relationships with both Western nations and sanctioned states. This balancing act highlights a shift toward a more multipolar world order, where countries prioritize their economic and strategic interests over ideological alignments.

The Rise of Regional Self-Reliance

Sanctions have exposed the vulnerabilities of over-dependence on global trade networks, prompting regions to invest in self-sufficiency and strengthen local economies.

Europe's Drive for Energy Independence: Europe's heavy reliance on Russian energy prior to the war has prompted a rapid diversification of energy sources. Investments in renewable energy, LNG infrastructure, and partnerships with non-Russian suppliers have accelerated, reflecting a broader push for energy security and independence from geopolitically unstable sources.

Local Manufacturing and Agriculture: Nations are prioritizing domestic production to mitigate the risks of external disruptions. Russia, for instance, has expanded its agricultural and manufacturing sectors to replace Western imports. Similar trends are visible in other regions, where localized supply chains are being developed to ensure economic resilience.

Regional Trade Agreements Gaining Traction: Agreements like the African Continental Free Trade Area (AfCFTA) and the Comprehensive and Progressive Agreement for Trans-Pacific Partnership (CPTPP) have gained renewed importance. These frameworks aim to enhance intra-regional trade, reduce external dependencies, and foster economic stability through collective growth.

Toward a Fragmented Yet Interconnected Global Order

The realignment of alliances in the wake of sanctions demonstrates the profound geopolitical consequences of economic measures. Traditional partnerships are being redefined, and emerging blocs are challenging the dominance of long-established powers. While this fragmentation may create competing spheres of influence, it also underscores the interconnectedness of global economies.

Multipolar Power Structures: The rise of alternative alliances and economic blocs reflects the emergence of a multipolar global order. Nations are increasingly pursuing diversified strategies to protect their interests, creating a complex and dynamic landscape.

Lessons in Resilience and Adaptation: The shifts in alliances underscore the importance of adaptability in a volatile world. By prioritizing regional self-reliance, diversifying partnerships, and fostering collaborative solutions, nations are better positioned to navigate future crises.

In conclusion, 'the realignment of global alliances triggered by sanctions during the Russia-Ukraine conflict illustrates how economic measures can reshape the geopolitical landscape. While sanctions isolate targeted nations, they also catalyze broader shifts in trade, finance, and international relations. As the world moves toward a more fragmented yet interconnected order, the focus will increasingly be on balancing competition with cooperation to build a resilient and equitable global system.

7.4 Shifting Trade Dependencies

The Russia-Ukraine war and the associated sanctions on Russia have acted as a seismic force, reshaping global trade dynamics and compelling nations to rethink their trade dependencies. These disruptions have underscored the fragility of over-reliance on specific partners or supply chains and have driven a widespread pivot toward diversification, technological innovation, and resilience-building. The adjustments made during this period reflect the adaptability of global economies and offer insights into the strategies needed to weather future crises.

Diversifying Import and Export Channels

One of the most immediate responses to disrupted trade routes has been a concerted effort by nations to diversify their import and export dependencies, ensuring greater stability in their trade networks.

Energy Supplies: Europe, once heavily reliant on Russian natural gas, has been at the forefront of diversification efforts. Countries have significantly ramped up imports of liquefied natural gas (LNG) from the United States, Qatar, and other producers, while accelerating investments in renewable energy projects like offshore wind and solar farms. These efforts aim not only to fill the energy gap but also to reduce vulnerabilities to future geopolitical shocks.

Agricultural Commodities: The loss of Ukrainian grain exports has driven nations to seek new agricultural trade relationships with countries in South America, Africa, and Asia. For instance, Brazil and Argentina have increased grain exports to regions like the Middle East and North Africa, reinforcing their roles as alternative suppliers in global food markets. These partnerships have also encouraged investment in agricultural infrastructure and logistics in these regions.

Redirection of Russian Exports: Facing Western sanctions, Russia has turned to alternative markets in Asia, the Middle East, and Africa. Discounted oil and gas exports to China and India have become a lifeline for Russia's energy sector, while fertilizer exports have bolstered trade relationships with developing nations reliant on agricultural inputs. This pivot reflects Russia's efforts to maintain economic activity despite its reduced access to traditional markets.

The Role of Technology in Circumventing Trade Barriers

Technological advancements have played a critical role in enabling nations and businesses to adapt to trade restrictions and ensure continuity in global commerce.

Financial Technologies: The exclusion of Russian banks from the SWIFT financial messaging system spurred the development and adoption of alternative systems like Russia's SPFS (System for Transfer of Financial Messages) and China's CIPS (Cross-Border Interbank Payment System). These platforms have facilitated continued international transactions, offering a glimpse into the future of decentralized financial systems.

Cryptocurrencies and Digital Payments: Cryptocurrencies have emerged as a tool for bypassing traditional banking restrictions. While their volatility and regulatory concerns limit widespread adoption, digital currencies have allowed limited financial transactions in sanctioned economies, ensuring some level of economic activity.

Supply Chain Innovations: Advances in logistics technology and data analytics have enabled businesses to quickly adapt to disrupted supply chains. Digital platforms for trade management have streamlined the process of finding alternative suppliers and optimizing transport routes, minimizing delays and costs.

Lessons Learned: Building Resilient Trade Networks

The disruptions caused by the Russia-Ukraine conflict have highlighted critical vulnerabilities in global trade systems, prompting nations and businesses to adopt more robust and resilient approaches.

Reducing Over-Reliance on Single Sources: The crisis has emphasized the dangers of depending heavily on a single country or region for essential goods and resources. Diversifying suppliers and trade partners has become a central strategy, with nations forging new trade agreements to spread risk more evenly across global markets.

Strengthening Domestic Production: Investments in local industries have gained traction as countries work to reduce import dependencies. European nations, for example, are investing heavily in renewable energy projects to bolster domestic energy production, while Asian economies are focusing on building local semiconductor manufacturing capabilities to address global chip shortages.

Fostering Regional Trade Frameworks: Multilateral agreements and regional trade blocs, such as the African Continental Free Trade Area (AfCFTA) and the Comprehensive and Progressive Agreement for Trans-Pacific Partnership (CPTPP), are gaining prominence. These frameworks enhance economic interdependence within regions, providing a buffer against external disruptions and promoting collective resilience.

Toward a Resilient Global Trade Ecosystem

The shifting trade dependencies brought about by the Russia-Ukraine conflict underscore the dynamic nature of global commerce. While the immediate adjustments were driven by necessity, they also reflect long-term strategies aimed at reducing vulnerabilities and fostering resilience. The diversification of trade channels, adoption of advanced technologies, and prioritization of regional collaboration represent a blueprint for navigating future disruptions.

Adapting to New Realities: The adjustments made during this period have shown how global trade networks can evolve rapidly in response to crises. By leveraging innovation and fostering partnerships, nations and businesses have not only mitigated immediate risks but also strengthened their foundations for future growth.

Balancing Interdependence with Self-Reliance: As countries continue to embrace globalization, the importance of balancing interdependence with self-reliance has come into sharper focus. Building robust local industries alongside diversified international partnerships will be key to maintaining stability in an unpredictable world.

In conclusion, the trade disruptions and realignments caused by the Russia-Ukraine war offer valuable lessons in resilience and adaptability. By embracing these lessons, nations and businesses can prepare for a future where trade networks are not only more robust but also more equitable and sustainable.

7.5 Sanctions as a Geopolitical Tool: Lessons for the Future

Sanctions have remained a cornerstone of international diplomacy, enabling nations to apply economic and political pressure without engaging in direct military action. The Russia-Ukraine war, however, has exposed both the strengths and weaknesses of sanctions as a geopolitical tool. As the global community evaluates their use, key lessons emerge on how to enhance their effectiveness, mitigate unintended harm, and adapt them to the realities of a multipolar world. By balancing strategic goals with humanitarian considerations and fostering global cooperation, sanctions can evolve into a more refined instrument of statecraft.

Balancing Economic Pressure with Humanitarian Concerns

Sanctions, while intended to punish governments or compel policy changes, often have significant collateral effects, particularly on civilians and neighboring economies. Addressing these challenges requires a more targeted and compassionate approach.

Minimizing Civilian Impact: Economic sanctions frequently disrupt access to essentials such as food, medicine, and energy. Vulnerable populations, including children, the elderly, and those in rural areas, are disproportionately affected. Future sanctions must incorporate safeguards to ensure that essential goods and services remain accessible. Mechanisms such as pre-approved humanitarian corridors or agreements with neutral parties can reduce civilian suffering while maintaining pressure on targeted regimes.

Humanitarian Exemptions: Explicit exemptions for humanitarian aid, overseen by international organizations like the United Nations, can ensure that lifesaving assistance reaches those in need. For instance, clear guidelines allowing the shipment of medical supplies and food can alleviate civilian hardships without undermining the sanctions' primary objectives.

Mitigating Global Spillovers: Sanctions on major economic players like Russia often have ripple effects that destabilize global markets. Rising energy and food prices, driven by restricted trade, disproportionately affect developing nations already grappling with economic challenges. Preemptive measures, such as coordinated financial assistance and emergency food programs, can help buffer these secondary effects and maintain global stability.

Rethinking Sanctions in a Multipolar World

The global power structure is undergoing a transformation, with emerging economies and regional powers playing increasingly influential roles. This shift necessitates a reexamination of how sanctions are designed, implemented, and enforced.

Emergence of Sanction-Resistant Networks: Nations like Russia and China are actively developing alternative economic systems to bypass Western-led mechanisms such as SWIFT and the U.S. dollar. Initiatives like Russia's SPFS payment system and China's CIPS highlight the need for sanctions strategies that account for these evolving networks. Engaging these nations in dialogue about global trade and finance frameworks may reduce the effectiveness of such bypass systems in the long term.

Engaging Emerging Powers: Sanctions are most effective when enforced by a broad coalition. To ensure this, major economies must engage regional powers like India, Brazil, and South Africa, aligning their interests to create a unified front. This approach enhances the legitimacy of sanctions and reduces opportunities for circumvention.

Regional Adaptability: In an increasingly multipolar world, a one-size-fits-all approach to sanctions is unlikely to succeed. Strategies must be tailored to the unique geopolitical dynamics and economic structures of different regions. For example, measures targeting energy exports should consider regional dependencies, ensuring that alternative suppliers are readily available.

Building Global Frameworks for Targeted and Effective Sanction Policies

To address the shortcomings highlighted by the Russia-Ukraine conflict, the international community must prioritize the creation of comprehensive and coordinated sanction frameworks. These should emphasize precision, accountability, and multilateral cooperation.

Targeted Sanctions: Broad sanctions often cause widespread harm, affecting ordinary citizens more than the political elites they are intended to pressure. Precision measures, such as freezing the assets of government officials, oligarchs, and military leaders or imposing travel bans, can apply direct pressure on decision-makers while minimizing collateral damage.

Enhanced Multilateral Coordination: The success of sanctions depends on consistent enforcement across borders. Strengthening cooperation among international bodies, governments, and private sector actors—such as banks and shipping companies—can close loopholes and prevent evasion. Shared databases, synchronized enforcement timelines, and joint monitoring systems can enhance the effectiveness of sanctions.

Transparency and Accountability: Sanctions must be accompanied by clear criteria for their implementation, review, and removal. Regular assessments by independent organizations can evaluate their impact, ensuring that they remain focused on achieving strategic goals without causing prolonged harm to civilians. Public reporting of these assessments can build trust and maintain international support.

The Path Forward: Refining Sanctions for a Complex World

The Russia-Ukraine war has demonstrated the dual-edged nature of sanctions. While they can impose significant economic and political costs, their unintended consequences and limited capacity to drive immediate policy changes highlight the need for reform. Moving forward, the global community must:

Prioritize Collaboration: Sanctions will be most effective when implemented and enforced through multilateral efforts that include a diverse range of nations.

Incorporate Flexibility: Adapting sanctions to changing geopolitical conditions and minimizing harm to civilians can enhance their legitimacy and reduce resistance.

Leverage Technology: Advances in digital monitoring and blockchain can improve transparency and accountability, ensuring sanctions are applied precisely and effectively.

Align with Broader Goals: Sanctions should be part of a comprehensive strategy that includes diplomacy, humanitarian support, and long-term economic planning.

In conclusion, sanctions remain a powerful but imperfect tool in the arsenal of modern diplomacy. By learning from past experiences, including the complexities revealed during the Russia-Ukraine conflict, the international community can refine their use, ensuring they remain effective, ethical, and adaptable to the challenges of an evolving geopolitical landscape.

Chapter 8: A New Economic Order?

The Russia-Ukraine war has not only reshaped the geopolitical landscape but has also accelerated a profound transformation in the global economic order. As the conflict disrupted long-standing trade relationships and exposed the vulnerabilities of interdependent supply chains, nations began to rethink their economic strategies. The era of globalization, once defined by seamless integration and shared prosperity, is increasingly giving way to regionalization and economic fragmentation. This chapter explores the forces driving this shift, the emerging regional power centers, and the opportunities and challenges of navigating a more fragmented economic landscape. In a world where priorities are rapidly evolving, the quest for balance between resilience and cooperation has become more critical than ever.

8.1 Accelerating Economic Fragmentation

The Russia-Ukraine war has fundamentally altered the trajectory of the global economy, serving as a turning point in the movement from integration to fragmentation. In a world once celebrated for its interconnected trade networks and cooperative economic policies, the conflict has magnified vulnerabilities in globalization, compelling nations to rethink the risks of over-dependence on interdependent systems. This shift marks a decisive departure from the ideals of seamless global integration, steering nations toward self-reliance, regionalism, and controlled alliances.

The End of Economic Integration?

The war has disrupted decades of economic integration, particularly in Europe, where dependency on Russian energy supplies became a glaring liability. The conflict illuminated the dangers of relying on potentially adversarial nations for essential resources, forcing governments to recalibrate their economic strategies.

Rather than pursuing unfettered global trade, many nations have pivoted toward policies emphasizing domestic production, energy independence, and regional partnerships. Investments in renewable energy, localized supply chains, and industrial autonomy signal a growing retreat from traditional globalization. Countries are implementing export controls on critical goods like food, semiconductors, and rare earth minerals, reflecting a shift toward prioritizing national security over global interdependence.

This transformation has not been limited to trade alone. Financial markets, technology sectors, and geopolitical alliances have also adjusted to the new reality, where economic integration is tempered by the need to safeguard sovereignty and mitigate risks from future geopolitical upheavals.

Trade Barriers and Economic Decoupling

The proliferation of sanctions during the Russia-Ukraine war and subsequent retaliatory measures has fueled an unprecedented rise in trade barriers. Sanctions aimed at economically isolating Russia disrupted the flow of goods and services across multiple industries, from energy and food to advanced technology. In turn, Russia sought to bypass these restrictions by forging trade relationships with non-Western nations, including China, India, and Turkey.

This decoupling of economies has introduced stark divisions in global trade networks. Western countries have increasingly adopted "friendshoring" policies, favoring partnerships with nations that share similar political ideologies and values. The United States, for instance, has prioritized collaborations with allies in Europe, East Asia, and North America to create secure and reliable supply chains. Similarly, Europe's diversification away from Russian gas has led to stronger ties with energy-exporting nations like Qatar, Norway, and the United States.

While these strategies aim to enhance resilience and security, they carry the unintended consequence of deepening economic divides. Emerging markets, caught between rival blocs, risk becoming peripheral players in the global economy, and global trade flows may face inefficiencies and higher costs as nations pivot toward exclusivity in partnerships.

Geopolitics as a Driving Force in Global Markets

The war has underscored the influence of geopolitics on global markets, often eclipsing traditional economic considerations like cost efficiency and comparative advantage. Energy markets have experienced some of the most profound changes, with Europe's move to reduce dependency on Russian gas reshaping alliances and energy trade flows. This realignment has led to increased imports of liquefied natural gas (LNG) from Qatar, the United States, and Australia, marking a strategic pivot in global energy dynamics.

In addition, supply chain adjustments in critical sectors like semiconductors and rare earth minerals have been driven by geopolitical tensions. Governments and industries have prioritized strategic autonomy, leading to the development of localized production capabilities and the diversification of supply sources. For example, efforts to establish domestic semiconductor manufacturing hubs in the United States and Europe reflect a deliberate response to the vulnerabilities exposed by reliance on single-source suppliers like China or Taiwan.

Opportunities and Challenges in an Era of Fragmentation

While economic fragmentation poses significant risks, such as inefficiencies, higher costs, and reduced global cooperation, it also presents opportunities to build more robust and diversified systems. Nations are now focusing on resilience by fostering innovation, investing in sustainable technologies, and creating buffer capacities in critical industries.

Efforts to balance security with collaboration will be critical in shaping the future of the global economy. While fragmentation signals the end of one era, it also offers the chance to redefine economic relationships, encouraging adaptability, fairness, and long-term sustainability.

The Russia-Ukraine war has accelerated the movement toward economic fragmentation, challenging the foundations of globalization. This emerging paradigm reflects a world where economic security, strategic autonomy, and regional alliances increasingly dominate over the ideals of interconnected markets and shared prosperity. How nations navigate these shifting dynamics will determine whether the global economy can evolve into a more balanced and resilient system.

8.2 Regionalization vs. Globalization

The Russia-Ukraine war has sharpened the global focus on the structural dynamics of economies, accelerating a shift toward regionalization as an alternative to full-scale globalization. While globalization has been the cornerstone of economic growth and international trade for decades, its vulnerabilities—exposed by geopolitical tensions and supply chain disruptions—have prompted nations and corporations to reconsider their strategies. This evolving balance between regionalization and globalization reflects a world in transition, where proximity and security are increasingly prioritized alongside traditional economic efficiencies.

Global Supply Chains: From Efficiency to Vulnerability

For years, global supply chains were lauded for their ability to lower costs, optimize production, and foster international cooperation. However, the Russia-Ukraine war disrupted critical supply routes for essential commodities like energy, grain, and industrial inputs, revealing the fragility of these interconnected systems. The ripple effects were immediate and widespread, causing shortages, price surges, and production delays across industries from automotive to agriculture.

In response, nations and businesses have begun to shift their focus toward more localized supply chains. Practices like **"nearshoring"** (bringing production closer to domestic markets) and **"friendshoring"** (relocating operations to allied or politically stable countries) have gained traction. These strategies aim to enhance predictability and reduce exposure to geopolitical risks. While effective in improving resilience, these measures also challenge the cost-saving benefits and cooperative spirit traditionally associated with globalization.

Regional Trade Agreements: A Growing Force

As the world reconfigures its economic relationships, regional trade agreements (RTAs) have emerged as critical tools for fostering economic security and reducing reliance on distant or adversarial partners.

Europe's Integration Efforts: The European Union (EU) has deepened its internal trade networks, particularly in energy and supply chains, to minimize dependency on external suppliers like Russia. The EU's focus on renewable energy, cross-border infrastructure, and regional innovation highlights its commitment to a more self-sufficient economic model.

Asia's Expanding Partnerships: The **Regional Comprehensive Economic Partnership (RCEP)**, which includes major economies like China, Japan, and ASEAN members, is shaping one of the largest trade zones in the world. This agreement prioritizes regional trade flows, simplified regulations, and shared growth, making Asia a central hub for economic collaboration.

Africa's Unified Vision: Initiatives like the **African Continental Free Trade Area (AfCFTA)** aim to bolster intra-African trade, reduce dependence on global markets, and unlock the continent's economic potential. By prioritizing regional manufacturing and resource-sharing, Africa is positioning itself as a significant player in the evolving economic landscape.

These agreements offer tangible benefits, such as reduced transportation costs, streamlined customs procedures, and stronger regional diplomacy. However, their rise also raises concerns about the diminishing influence of global institutions like the **World Trade Organization (WTO)**, which historically aimed to mediate and facilitate global trade on a broader scale.

Balancing Regionalization and Globalization: Striking the Right Note

While the pivot toward regionalization provides greater resilience against disruptions, it is not without challenges. Overemphasis on localized systems can lead to inefficiencies, reduced competition, and higher production costs. Additionally, the exclusionary nature of some regional agreements may limit access to diverse markets and create new economic divides.

The key lies in balancing regionalization with the enduring strengths of globalization:

Dual Sourcing and Redundancy: Businesses are adopting strategies that involve sourcing from multiple regions to reduce dependency on single suppliers or markets. This approach balances cost efficiency with the flexibility to navigate disruptions.

Strategic Stockpiling and Buffer Systems: Industries are building reserves of critical materials and components to weather short-term supply chain shocks while continuing to engage in global trade.

Digital Supply Chain Innovations: Advanced technologies like **blockchain**, **predictive analytics**, and **real-time tracking systems** are helping industries enhance visibility, efficiency, and adaptability across supply chains.

Toward a Balanced Economic Framework

The ongoing debate between regionalization and globalization reflects a broader question: how can nations and businesses build an economic framework that fosters resilience without sacrificing growth and collaboration? The future likely lies in a hybrid approach—leveraging regionalization to strengthen local security and efficiency, while maintaining the benefits of global interconnectedness to drive innovation and shared prosperity.

This transition is not just a response to the immediate crises of the Russia-Ukraine war but a long-term reimagining of how the world conducts trade and builds economic partnerships. The choices made in this period of flux will define the shape of the global economy for decades, balancing resilience, inclusivity, and the enduring pursuit of growth.

8.3 Emerging Regional Powerhouses

The global economic disruptions triggered by the Russia-Ukraine war have accelerated a shift in the balance of power, ushering in an era where regional powerhouses play increasingly pivotal roles. This transition reflects the fragmentation of global economic structures, with regions like Asia, Africa, Latin America, and Europe asserting themselves as critical players in shaping a new, multipolar world order. These emerging centers of influence are not only adapting to the challenges of the current geopolitical climate but are also laying the groundwork for more resilient, self-reliant, and dynamic economic systems.

Asia's Expanding Economic Influence

Asia continues to solidify its position as the engine of global economic growth, leveraging its vast markets, strategic innovations, and geopolitical maneuvering to lead in a fragmented global landscape. The region's diversity of economies—from manufacturing giants to emerging tech hubs—underpins its growing dominance.

China's Strategic Dominance

China remains at the forefront as a manufacturing powerhouse and a leader in advanced technologies, renewable energy, and global infrastructure projects. Its **Belt and Road Initiative (BRI)** exemplifies its strategy to connect and control trade routes across Asia, Africa, and Europe. Despite facing scrutiny and geopolitical pushback, China has strengthened ties with nations seeking alternatives to Western-led economic frameworks, ensuring its continued influence in global markets.

India's Strategic Ascent

India has positioned itself as a key counterbalance to China, benefiting from its democratic credentials, burgeoning middle class, and expanding industrial base. The nation has capitalized on its relationships with Western economies, becoming a hub for **technology, pharmaceuticals, and services.** By actively participating in trade agreements like the **Regional Comprehensive Economic Partnership (RCEP)** and focusing on infrastructure development, India has bolstered its role as a cornerstone of Asia's economic resilience.

Southeast Asia's Regional Integration

Southeast Asia, through organizations like **ASEAN**, continues to grow as a regional hub for manufacturing, digital innovation, and trade. Countries like Vietnam, Indonesia, and Thailand have emerged as attractive destinations for foreign direct investment, thanks to their strategic locations and pro-business reforms. The region's focus on intra-Asian trade and partnerships reinforces its importance in a shifting economic landscape.

Africa and Latin America: The Next Frontiers

Africa and Latin America are increasingly recognized as critical players in the evolving global economy. Rich in natural resources and home to burgeoning markets, these regions are leveraging their assets to attract investment, diversify trade, and assert greater influence on the global stage.

Africa's Rising Potential

Africa's abundant resources and youthful population position it as a rising economic powerhouse. The **African Continental Free Trade Area (AfCFTA)** is a transformative initiative aimed at boosting intra-African trade, fostering industrialization, and reducing reliance on external markets. Africa's potential in **renewable energy, agriculture, and technology** is attracting interest from global powers seeking to diversify supply chains and secure access to essential commodities.

Key industries, such as **solar and wind energy projects**, are gaining traction, particularly as countries pivot toward greener economies. Moreover, Africa's strategic geographic position—bridging key trade routes between Europe, Asia, and the Americas—further enhances its global relevance.

Latin America's Green Revolution

Latin America is emerging as a key supplier of critical commodities essential for the green transition. Nations like **Chile, Argentina, and Brazil** are leading in the production of lithium, copper, and other materials vital for renewable energy technologies and electric vehicles. These industries are driving economic growth and positioning Latin America as an indispensable player in the global shift toward sustainability.

Additionally, Latin America's geographic proximity to North America provides a strategic advantage for **nearshoring initiatives**, enabling faster, more cost-effective supply chain solutions. The region's focus on digital transformation and sustainable agriculture further enhances its role in the fragmented global economy.

Europe's Pursuit of Strategic Autonomy

The Russia-Ukraine war has galvanized Europe's efforts to enhance its economic and political independence. Confronted with an energy crisis and supply chain vulnerabilities, the European Union (EU) has prioritized investments in **renewable energy, strategic industries, and defense.**

Energy Transition

Europe's urgent need to reduce reliance on Russian gas has accelerated the shift toward **renewable energy projects** and diversified energy partnerships. Investments in solar, wind, and hydrogen technologies are reshaping the continent's energy landscape, while collaborations with energy-rich nations like Norway and Qatar ensure supply stability.

Technological Leadership

The EU is doubling down on **semiconductor manufacturing, pharmaceutical production, and digital innovation** to secure its place in critical global industries. By fostering research and development, the bloc is building resilience against external shocks and establishing itself as a leader in sustainable economic practices.

Global Advocacy for Sustainability

Europe's leadership in climate action and sustainable development positions it as a global advocate for green initiatives. Partnerships with Africa, Asia, and Latin America in clean energy and technology are helping to drive shared progress while reducing dependency on traditional economic superpowers.

Toward a Multipolar Economic Order

The rise of regional powerhouses signals the emergence of a multipolar global economy, where influence and opportunities are distributed across diverse centers of growth. These regions, with their distinct strengths and strategies, are challenging the dominance of traditional economic powers and reshaping the future of global trade and cooperation.

Asia's Innovation and Scale: Asia's industrial capacity and technological advancements ensure its continued leadership in global markets.

Africa and Latin America's Resources: These regions' natural wealth and emerging markets offer new opportunities for investment and sustainable development.

Europe's Strategic Resilience: The EU's focus on autonomy and sustainability sets a benchmark for balancing economic security with global collaboration.

Together, these regional powerhouses are driving a more inclusive and adaptive economic framework, one that reflects the complexities of a fragmented yet interconnected world. As they rise to prominence, they offer a blueprint for navigating global challenges while fostering long-term growth and stability.

8.4 Opportunities and Challenges in a Fragmented World

The fragmentation of the global economy, fueled by geopolitical upheavals and disruptions such as the Russia-Ukraine war, marks a transformative period with profound implications. While the move toward regionalization offers opportunities for localized growth and innovation, it also raises significant challenges that test the resilience and adaptability of nations. Successfully navigating this fragmented landscape requires a blend of strategic regional initiatives and sustained global cooperation.

Opportunities: Innovation and Regional Resilience

The pivot toward regionalization is fostering new opportunities for economic development, technological progress, and collaboration, particularly in areas where localized approaches are proving effective.

Localized Technological Development

The disruption of global supply chains has prompted regions to prioritize self-reliance by investing in local manufacturing and research. This trend is spurring advancements in critical sectors:

Renewable Energy: Countries like India and China are leading in solar and wind energy innovations, while Europe is heavily investing in green hydrogen projects.

Advanced Manufacturing: Asia's industrial hubs, such as Vietnam and South Korea, are enhancing their manufacturing capabilities through automation and AI-driven solutions, reducing reliance on global supply chains.

Digital Infrastructure: Regions across Africa are adopting fintech innovations to improve financial inclusion, with mobile payment platforms and blockchain technology revolutionizing local economies.

Cross-Sector Collaboration

Regional initiatives are pooling resources and expertise to address shared challenges:

Agriculture in Africa: The African Continental Free Trade Area (AfCFTA) is driving innovation in sustainable farming, improving food security, and enabling cross-border trade.

Sustainable Mining in Latin America: Countries like Chile and Bolivia are capitalizing on their rich lithium reserves to support the global shift to electric vehicles, fostering partnerships with international corporations.

Opportunities for SMEs and Startups

Localized economies are proving fertile ground for small and medium enterprises (SMEs) and startups:

Governments are introducing targeted incentives, such as tax breaks and funding programs, to stimulate innovation and fill gaps in disrupted supply chains.

Startups are emerging as leaders in niche markets, from agri-tech in Sub-Saharan Africa to AI and IoT solutions in Southeast Asia.

Challenges: Risks of Isolationism and Inequality

While the emphasis on regionalization brings opportunities, it also risks deepening divisions and creating vulnerabilities that could hinder global progress.

Trade Protectionism

The focus on self-reliance has led to the resurgence of protectionist policies:

Tariffs and Export Controls: Nations are imposing restrictions on key goods like food, technology, and energy to safeguard domestic interests, which can escalate trade tensions.

Barriers to Foreign Investment: Protectionist measures may deter international investors, limiting access to capital for developing nations.

Economic Inequality

The benefits of regionalization are not equally distributed:

Wealthier regions with advanced infrastructure and technological capabilities can adapt more effectively, leaving less-developed areas at risk of marginalization.

Countries without resources to diversify their economies may face prolonged stagnation, widening global inequalities.

Geopolitical Tensions

Economic isolationism can exacerbate political divides:

Regional Rivalries: Competing interests among neighboring countries can undermine collaborative efforts and spark conflicts.

Diplomatic Stalemates: As nations focus inward, resolving global challenges like climate change and health crises becomes increasingly difficult.

Building Bridges: Strategies for Inclusive Growth

To harness the opportunities and address the challenges of a fragmented world, nations must adopt innovative strategies that balance regionalization with global collaboration.

Strengthening Regional Cooperation

Regional alliances provide a framework for collective growth:

Intra-Regional Trade: Agreements like ASEAN, MERCOSUR, and AfCFTA promote economic integration, enhance market access, and reduce trade barriers.

Resource Sharing: Collaborative energy grids, shared water resources, and joint infrastructure projects strengthen resilience and foster interdependence.

Engaging in Multilateral Dialogue

Global issues require solutions that transcend regional boundaries:

Climate Action: Coordinated efforts through international agreements, such as the Paris Accord, ensure shared responsibility for sustainability.

Pandemic Preparedness: Unified health strategies can mitigate the risks of future global health crises.

Fostering Economic and Technological Resilience

Nations can strengthen their economies and mitigate risks through:

Diversified Supply Chains: Balancing local production with global trade partnerships reduces vulnerability to regional disruptions.

Innovation Networks: Collaborative research and development (R&D) initiatives across borders accelerate technological progress, addressing shared challenges like energy transition and cybersecurity.

Promoting Inclusivity and Equity

Ensuring that the benefits of regionalization are widely shared is critical:

Developing targeted programs to support marginalized regions and communities can bridge gaps in wealth and access.

Supporting vocational training and education initiatives equips populations with the skills needed to thrive in new economic realities.

A Reimagined Global Framework

The shift toward regionalization does not signal the end of globalization but rather its evolution into a more adaptable and inclusive model. The challenge lies in integrating regional strengths into a broader global framework that fosters stability, collaboration, and sustainable growth.

Regional Strengths: Leveraging localized innovations and resources to build economic resilience.

Global Cooperation: Maintaining dialogue and partnerships to address cross-border challenges and ensure equitable development.

By embracing these strategies, the international community can transform fragmentation into an opportunity for reinvention, ensuring that the global economy evolves to meet the demands of a dynamic and interconnected world.

8.5 Lessons for the Future: Toward a Balanced Economic Order

The economic fragmentation intensified by the Russia-Ukraine war highlights critical lessons for fostering a sustainable and resilient global economy. The challenges of a multipolar world call for a balanced economic order that integrates the strengths of regionalization with the interconnected benefits of globalization. By adopting a hybrid approach rooted in collaboration, innovation, and adaptability, the global community can address shared challenges while ensuring equitable growth.

Embracing Hybrid Models: Integrating Regional and Global Strengths

The rigid dichotomy between globalization and regionalization no longer serves the complexities of today's economic realities. Instead, a blended model offers the flexibility and resilience needed to navigate future disruptions.

Regional Foundations with Global Connectivity

Strengthened Regional Hubs: Nations are investing in regional supply chains to minimize vulnerabilities from global disruptions. Southeast Asia's manufacturing ecosystems and Africa's emerging trade blocs exemplify this approach.

Global Trade Integration: While prioritizing regional resilience, countries are maintaining open channels for global markets. For example,

Europe's regional energy strategies coexist with its international trade partnerships.

Flexibility in Trade Relationships

Diversified Agreements: Establishing multiple trade relationships across regions reduces dependency on single partners, fostering resilience. Agreements like the African Continental Free Trade Area (AfCFTA) demonstrate how regional alliances can complement global trade.

Dynamic Market Engagement: Nations are adopting adaptive strategies that allow them to participate in both regional and global markets, balancing immediate needs with long-term growth opportunities.

Technological Connectivity as a Bridge

Digital Infrastructure: Innovations like blockchain, AI-driven supply chain management, and cloud-based collaboration tools enhance the integration of regional and global economic systems.

Data-Driven Insights: Shared technology platforms allow regions to streamline logistics, monitor trade flows, and optimize production, creating efficiencies that benefit both local and international stakeholders.

Collaborative Solutions for Shared Challenges

Global challenges such as climate change, public health, and digital security demand collective action that transcends economic fragmentation.

Climate-Resilient Economies

Joint Green Investments: Collaborative funding for renewable energy, carbon capture, and sustainable agriculture can unite global and regional efforts to combat climate change.

Shared Resource Management: Cross-border initiatives, such as river basin management and renewable energy grids, demonstrate the power of regional collaboration for global environmental goals.

Strengthening Health Security

Regional Vaccine Hubs: The COVID-19 pandemic underscored the importance of localized production for equitable vaccine distribution. Partnerships like COVAX show how global frameworks can enhance regional capabilities.

Equitable Health Access: Establishing cooperative networks for research, manufacturing, and distribution ensures preparedness for future pandemics and health crises.

Digital Governance

Harmonizing Standards: Global agreements on data privacy, cybersecurity, and e-commerce are essential for fostering trust in digital trade.

Collaborative Technology Development: Joint efforts in developing AI, cybersecurity frameworks, and quantum computing technologies ensure inclusive participation in the digital economy.

Reimagining Partnerships in a Multipolar World

The transition to a multipolar economic landscape calls for a new vision of cooperation, emphasizing inclusivity, equity, and mutual growth.

Inclusive Multilateral Institutions

Broader Representation: Expanding the role of emerging economies in global decision-making bodies like the World Trade Organization (WTO) and International Monetary Fund (IMF) strengthens their relevance and effectiveness.

Equitable Policy Development: Multilateral institutions must balance the interests of developed and developing nations, ensuring fair outcomes for all participants.

South-South Cooperation

Emerging Economy Alliances: Collaboration between Africa, Latin America, and Asia showcases the potential for mutual growth through shared infrastructure, technology, and trade projects.

Resource-Sharing Frameworks: Partnerships focused on leveraging regional resources, such as renewable energy and agricultural innovation, amplify the voices of developing nations.

Private-Public Partnerships

Collaborative Investments: Governments and private enterprises can work together to address economic challenges, from infrastructure development to digital transformation.

Innovation and Growth: Public funding paired with private sector expertise accelerates the adoption of new technologies and enhances economic resilience.

A Vision for Balanced Economic Leadership

The lessons of the Russia-Ukraine war emphasize the importance of adaptability and collaboration in building a resilient global economic order. By integrating regional strengths with global cooperation, the international community can create a framework that prioritizes:

Cooperation Over Competition: Encouraging partnerships that transcend geopolitical divides.

Innovation Over Isolation: Leveraging technology to connect regions while fostering local resilience.

Shared Prosperity Over Division: Ensuring inclusive growth through equitable policies and investments.

This balanced economic order offers a pathway toward sustainability, equity, and unity in an increasingly complex world. By learning from the disruptions of the past and investing in collaborative, forward-thinking strategies, nations can forge a resilient and inclusive global economy for future generations.

Chapter 9: Lessons and Recommendations

The Russia-Ukraine war has served as a stark reminder of the vulnerabilities and interdependencies within the global economic system. The conflict has exposed critical weaknesses in supply chains, energy security, and international cooperation, while simultaneously underscoring the resilience and adaptability of nations and industries. As the world navigates the aftershocks of this geopolitical crisis, it is essential to draw actionable lessons that can inform policies, strategies, and frameworks for the future. This chapter synthesizes these lessons, offering recommendations to build resilient economies, diversify critical resources, and strengthen global alliances in an era marked by uncertainty and fragmentation. By addressing these challenges with a forward-looking approach, the global community can lay the foundation for a more stable, inclusive, and sustainable economic order.

9.1 Building Resilient Economies for the Future

The Russia-Ukraine war has underscored the critical need for nations to cultivate resilience within their economies to withstand and adapt to geopolitical disruptions, supply chain breakdowns, and unforeseen crises. Building resilient economies involves not just addressing immediate vulnerabilities but also preparing for long-term challenges through strategic planning, innovation, and international collaboration. Below are the key pillars for fostering resilience in economic systems.

Prioritizing Economic Flexibility and Adaptability

Flexibility and adaptability are essential for economies to respond effectively to sudden disruptions, whether they stem from conflict, natural disasters, or global health emergencies. Nations must focus on developing economic structures that can pivot quickly in the face of adversity.

Dynamic Policy Frameworks: Governments should adopt flexible policy frameworks that allow for rapid adjustments in response to evolving circumstances. For instance, fiscal and monetary policies should be designed to balance short-term recovery needs with long-term growth objectives.

Diversification of Economic Activities: Over-reliance on specific industries or export markets creates vulnerabilities. By fostering a diverse economic base—including agriculture, technology, manufacturing, and services—countries can reduce exposure to sector-specific shocks.

Encouraging Small and Medium Enterprises (SMEs): SMEs play a crucial role in maintaining economic stability during crises. Supporting these businesses through financial incentives, streamlined regulations, and access to technology can enhance economic adaptability and job creation.

Enhancing Domestic Manufacturing and Self-Reliance

The disruptions caused by the war have demonstrated the risks of excessive dependence on global supply chains. Enhancing domestic manufacturing and promoting self-reliance in critical sectors can strengthen economic stability while fostering innovation and local job creation.

Strategic Investments in Manufacturing: Governments and private sectors should prioritize investments in manufacturing capabilities, particularly in industries critical to national security, such as pharmaceuticals, semiconductors, and renewable energy technologies.

Strengthening Food and Energy Security: Self-sufficiency in food production and energy generation is vital for resilience. Initiatives like urban farming, renewable energy projects, and local processing facilities can reduce dependence on volatile global markets.

Public-Private Partnerships: Collaboration between governments and industries can accelerate the development of domestic capabilities. Incentives such as tax breaks, grants, and low-interest loans can encourage private investment in infrastructure and technology.

Leveraging Technology for Crisis Management and Economic Stability

Technological advancements play a pivotal role in enabling economies to anticipate, manage, and recover from crises. By harnessing the power of digital tools, nations can enhance both their preparedness and their long-term economic resilience.

Predictive Analytics and Data-Driven Decision-Making: Governments and businesses can utilize big data and predictive analytics to monitor global trends, forecast potential disruptions, and plan preemptive measures. For example, early-warning systems for supply chain disruptions can help industries mitigate risks proactively.

Digital Transformation of Public Services: The integration of digital platforms in governance—such as e-governance and digital payment systems—can ensure the continuity of essential services during crises and improve transparency and efficiency in resource allocation.

Encouraging Innovation in Crisis Technologies: Investments in technologies like blockchain for supply chain management, AI for resource optimization, and advanced logistics systems can strengthen economic stability during periods of uncertainty.

Promoting Education and Skill Development: A tech-savvy workforce is essential for leveraging the potential of digital tools. Vocational training and upskilling programs should focus on equipping workers with the competencies needed for emerging industries and technologies.

The Path Ahead

Building resilient economies requires a multi-faceted approach that balances immediate crisis responses with long-term sustainability. By fostering economic flexibility, enhancing domestic capabilities, and embracing technology, nations can create robust systems capable of thriving in an increasingly volatile global environment. Resilience is not just a strategy for survival; it is a blueprint for progress and stability in an interconnected world.

9.2 Diversifying Energy, Food, and Trade Sources

The Russia-Ukraine war has highlighted the vulnerabilities inherent in over-reliance on single suppliers or regions for critical resources such as energy, food, and trade. Diversification across these domains is essential for mitigating risks, enhancing resilience, and ensuring long-term sustainability. A robust approach to diversification includes reducing dependence on centralized sources, investing in renewable energy, encouraging agricultural innovation, and strengthening supply chain structures.

Reducing Dependence on Single Suppliers or Regions

Dependence on single suppliers or regions creates systemic vulnerabilities that can lead to economic instability during disruptions. Diversification strategies are crucial to safeguarding against such risks.

Developing Alternative Energy Sources: Nations heavily reliant on Russian gas or Middle Eastern oil have faced severe energy shocks during the war. Expanding partnerships with multiple energy suppliers and investing in diverse energy technologies, such as nuclear, wind, and geothermal, can create a balanced energy mix.

Diversifying Trade Partners: Countries must broaden their trading relationships to reduce exposure to regional conflicts or geopolitical tensions. Engaging with emerging markets in Africa, Latin America, and Southeast Asia can open new avenues for trade and investment.

Fostering Regional Collaboration: Strengthening regional trade agreements and economic alliances, such as the African Continental Free Trade Area (AfCFTA) or the Comprehensive and Progressive Agreement for Trans-Pacific Partnership (CPTPP), can help nations develop mutually beneficial partnerships and reduce dependence on global networks.

Expanding Renewable Energy Investments and Infrastructure

The energy crisis triggered by the war underscores the urgency of transitioning to renewable energy sources. Expanding investments in sustainable energy infrastructure not only reduces reliance on fossil fuels but also contributes to environmental sustainability.

Scaling Up Renewable Energy Projects: Governments should prioritize investments in solar, wind, and hydropower projects to enhance energy independence. Large-scale projects, such as offshore wind farms and solar parks, can cater to both domestic and export markets.

Modernizing Energy Grids: The integration of smart grid technologies ensures efficient distribution and storage of renewable energy. These grids can also support decentralized energy generation, reducing the risk of large-scale outages.

Public and Private Sector Collaboration: Partnerships between governments and private companies can accelerate the development of renewable energy infrastructure. Incentives like subsidies, tax breaks, and low-interest loans can encourage private sector investment.

Energy Storage Solutions: Investing in advanced energy storage technologies, such as battery systems and hydrogen solutions, can address the intermittency of renewable energy sources, ensuring a steady and reliable power supply.

Encouraging Agricultural Innovation and Food Security Programs

The disruption of grain and fertilizer exports during the conflict has highlighted the importance of resilient agricultural systems. Innovations in farming and robust food security programs are essential to mitigate the risks of global food crises.

Investing in Agricultural Technology: Precision farming, drones, and AI-powered analytics can enhance productivity and resource management in agriculture. These technologies enable farmers to optimize water usage, soil health, and crop yields.

Promoting Climate-Resilient Crops: Developing and distributing drought-tolerant, disease-resistant crop varieties can help countries adapt to changing environmental conditions and reduce dependence on imports.

Strengthening Local Food Systems: Encouraging urban farming, community-supported agriculture (CSA), and local food cooperatives can enhance food self-sufficiency and reduce reliance on global supply chains.

Implementing Comprehensive Food Security Policies: Governments should develop policies that ensure equitable access to food, support smallholder farmers, and build strategic grain reserves to safeguard against supply disruptions.

Strengthening Supply Chain Resilience and Redundancy

The disruption of global supply chains during the war emphasized the need for resilience and redundancy to ensure the smooth flow of goods and services.

Building Redundant Supply Chains: Establishing multiple supply routes and suppliers for critical goods reduces dependency on single points of failure. For example, sourcing raw materials from diverse regions can ensure continuity in manufacturing processes.

Adopting Digital Supply Chain Technologies: Blockchain, AI, and IoT can provide real-time visibility and predictive analytics for supply chain management. These tools help businesses anticipate disruptions and take proactive measures to mitigate them.

Enhancing Local Manufacturing Capacities: Investing in domestic production capabilities for essential goods, such as pharmaceuticals and semiconductors, reduces vulnerability to global supply chain shocks.

Encouraging Regional Logistics Hubs: Developing regional hubs for warehousing and distribution ensures faster and more reliable delivery of goods, particularly during crises.

The Path Forward

Diversifying energy, food, and trade sources is not just a strategic necessity but a foundation for economic resilience and sustainability. By reducing dependencies, fostering innovation, and strengthening supply chains, nations can build systems that withstand shocks while fostering equitable and inclusive growth. This approach ensures that future disruptions—whether geopolitical, economic, or environmental—are met with stability and preparedness, securing the well-being of populations and economies alike.

9.3 Strengthening International Economic Cooperation and Alliances

The interconnected challenges of the modern world, amplified by the disruptions of the Russia-Ukraine war, underscore the urgent need for enhanced international economic cooperation and strategic alliances. Strengthening global partnerships is crucial for addressing shared vulnerabilities, promoting sustainable growth, and fostering resilience in an increasingly fragmented economic landscape. By reinforcing multilateral institutions, advancing regional trade agreements, aligning policies on global priorities, and leveraging public-private collaborations, nations can chart a path toward a more stable and inclusive future.

Reinforcing Multilateral Institutions for Global Stability

Multilateral institutions play a pivotal role in maintaining global stability by facilitating dialogue, coordinating policies, and addressing systemic risks. Strengthening these organizations ensures that collective action can effectively tackle complex challenges.

Revitalizing Global Institutions: Institutions like the World Trade Organization (WTO), International Monetary Fund (IMF), and World Bank must adapt to the realities of a multipolar world. Ensuring that emerging economies have a stronger voice in these bodies fosters legitimacy and enhances global cooperation.

Strengthening Crisis-Response Mechanisms: Multilateral organizations need robust frameworks to respond swiftly to crises, such as pandemics or economic disruptions. Establishing global contingency funds and streamlined decision-making processes can enhance their effectiveness.

Addressing Inequality in Global Governance: Equitable representation in multilateral forums ensures that the interests of developing nations are adequately addressed, fostering trust and participation in collective initiatives.

Promoting Regional Trade Agreements for Shared Growth

Regional trade agreements are essential for fostering economic integration, enhancing regional self-reliance, and building resilience against global disruptions. They serve as vital platforms for shared growth and cooperation.

Expanding Existing Agreements: Agreements like the African Continental Free Trade Area (AfCFTA), the Comprehensive and Progressive Agreement for Trans-Pacific Partnership (CPTPP), and ASEAN Free Trade

Area (AFTA) offer models for boosting intra-regional trade and investment. Expanding their scope and membership can amplify their impact.

Encouraging Inclusive Frameworks: Trade agreements should include provisions that benefit small and medium enterprises (SMEs), women-led businesses, and underserved communities, ensuring equitable access to economic opportunities.

Streamlining Trade Regulations: Simplifying customs procedures, reducing tariffs, and harmonizing standards within regional blocs can remove barriers to trade and increase efficiency, boosting economic activity.

Aligning Policies for Climate Change, Health, and Digital Governance

Global challenges like climate change, health crises, and digital transformation transcend national borders, requiring coordinated policy responses and shared standards.

Coordinating Climate Action: International cooperation on carbon pricing, renewable energy investments, and green technology transfers is essential for achieving climate goals. Joint initiatives, such as global carbon markets and climate adaptation funds, can accelerate the transition to sustainable economies.

Strengthening Global Health Governance: The COVID-19 pandemic underscored the importance of unified health strategies. Establishing regional vaccine production hubs, improving global disease surveillance, and ensuring equitable access to healthcare resources are critical priorities.

Harmonizing Digital Policies: As digital economies expand, aligning policies on data privacy, cybersecurity, and digital trade is essential. Developing global standards ensures trust and facilitates seamless cross-border digital interactions, benefiting businesses and consumers alike.

Bridging Divides Through Public-Private Partnerships

Public-private partnerships (PPPs) are instrumental in addressing the resource and expertise gaps in global challenges. By fostering collaboration between governments, businesses, and civil society, PPPs can drive innovation and mobilize resources effectively.

Infrastructure Development: Governments can collaborate with private entities to develop critical infrastructure, such as renewable energy plants, transportation networks, and digital connectivity hubs, accelerating development and creating jobs.

Innovation in Public Services: Partnerships with technology firms can improve public services, such as healthcare, education, and disaster management, through the adoption of AI, IoT, and cloud-based solutions.

Financing Sustainable Development: Blended financing models, combining public funds with private investments, can support large-scale projects that address climate change, poverty reduction, and urbanization challenges.

The Path Forward

Strengthening international economic cooperation and alliances is central to navigating the complexities of a fragmented world. By reinforcing multilateral institutions, advancing regional integration, aligning policies on global challenges, and leveraging the strengths of public-private partnerships, nations can build a more resilient and inclusive global economy. These measures emphasize collaboration over division, creating a framework for shared prosperity, stability, and sustainable development in the face of future crises.

Appendices

Appendix A: Timeline of the Russia-Ukraine War and Global Economic Impacts

This timeline provides a chronological overview of the major events of the Russia-Ukraine war, along with its economic and geopolitical ripple effects.

1. **February 2022**: Russia's invasion of Ukraine sparks immediate global condemnation and initial sanctions.
2. **March 2022**: Energy markets destabilize as Europe seeks alternatives to Russian gas.
3. **April 2022**: Grain exports from Ukraine fall sharply due to blockades, intensifying global food crises.
4. **July 2022**: The EU launches REPowerEU to accelerate renewable energy adoption.
5. **November 2022**: Sanctions expand to Russian oil, impacting global markets.
6. **2023**: Supply chain realignments and regional trade agreements accelerate globally.

Appendix B: Key Data and Statistics

This appendix delves into the detailed numerical and visual representations of the critical data points discussed throughout the book, offering readers a factual basis for understanding the economic impacts of the Russia-Ukraine conflict. The statistics highlight key aspects of energy markets, commodity prices, inflation trends, and trade realignments.

1. Energy Market Dynamics

Changes in Oil and Gas Prices from February 2022 Onward

- **Oil Prices:** The war caused Brent crude oil prices to surge dramatically, crossing $130 per barrel in March 2022, up from approximately $80 per barrel in December 2021. This marked a near 63% increase within a few months. The global average price of gasoline rose in parallel, reaching record highs in many countries, including the United States, where prices surpassed $5 per gallon in mid-2022.
- **Natural Gas Prices:** European natural gas prices, represented by the Dutch TTF benchmark, skyrocketed to €340 per megawatt-hour in August 2022, a staggering 400% increase from €65 in early 2021. The crisis prompted urgent measures to diversify gas supplies.

Europe's Energy Import Diversification Efforts

- **Reduction in Russian Gas Dependency:** Before the war, Russia supplied over 40% of Europe's natural gas. By late 2022, this reliance had dropped to below 15%, as countries diversified imports, increasing liquefied natural gas (LNG) purchases from the United States and Qatar. Germany, for instance, constructed LNG terminals in record time, with two operational by early 2023.
- **Renewables Expansion:** Renewable energy capacity in Europe surged. By the end of 2022, the European Union added 57 GW of

wind and solar capacity, a 25% increase compared to the previous year.

2. Commodity Price Fluctuations

Wheat, Corn, and Sunflower Oil Price Trends During the Conflict

- **Wheat:** Wheat prices spiked to $13 per bushel in May 2022, a 65% increase compared to $7.50 per bushel in mid-2021. Major importers in the Middle East and Africa faced acute shortages and soaring food prices.
- **Corn:** Corn prices rose from $5.90 per bushel in January 2022 to $8 per bushel by mid-2022, significantly affecting livestock feed costs and global food prices.
- **Sunflower Oil:** Ukraine's status as the largest global exporter of sunflower oil meant disruptions drove prices up by 75% globally. By May 2022, the price of sunflower oil reached $2,300 per metric ton, compared to $1,300 in 2021.

3. Inflation and Currency Volatility

Regional Inflation Trends Across Europe, Africa, Asia, and the Americas

- **Europe:** Inflation rates in the Eurozone climbed to a historic 10.6% in October 2022, driven by soaring energy prices. Baltic states like Estonia faced inflation exceeding 20%.
- **Africa:** Food price inflation surged across Africa, with nations like Zimbabwe experiencing inflation rates above 250% by mid-2022, exacerbating poverty and hunger.
- **Asia:** Emerging economies in Asia, such as Sri Lanka, saw inflation rise to 70% in 2022, driven by food and fuel shortages.
- **Americas:** The United States experienced inflation peaking at 9.1% in June 2022, the highest in four decades, largely driven by energy and food costs.

Depreciation of Currencies in Emerging Economies

- **Turkish Lira:** The Turkish lira lost 28% of its value in 2022 due to inflationary pressures and increased energy import costs.
- **Egyptian Pound:** The Egyptian pound depreciated by over 35% in 2022, following disruptions in wheat imports from Ukraine, a primary supplier.
- **Sri Lankan Rupee:** Sri Lanka's rupee saw a 45% depreciation amid its economic crisis, leading to widespread shortages of essential goods.

4. Trade Realignments

Growth of Trade with Non-Western Partners in Sanctioned Economies

- **Russia's Pivot to Asia:** Russian energy exports to China and India rose sharply. By 2023, China became Russia's largest oil importer, with daily imports exceeding 2 million barrels, up from 1.5 million barrels in early 2022. Indian imports of discounted Russian crude increased 400% year-on-year.
- **Middle Eastern Trade Expansion:** Russia expanded trade with Middle Eastern countries, including significant increases in agricultural exports to Turkey and Iran.
- **African Partnerships:** Africa's imports of Russian fertilizer and grain rose by 20% in 2022, as countries like Algeria and Egypt sought to secure affordable alternatives amid Western market volatility.

Appendix C: In-Depth Case Studies

This appendix provides detailed analyses of specific instances that illustrate the broader themes explored in the book. These case studies highlight the real-world implications of global economic shifts and geopolitical disruptions, offering a closer look at how different regions and nations have navigated these challenges.

Case Study 1: Europe's Energy Transition Amid Crisis

Overview:

Europe's response to the energy crisis triggered by the Russia-Ukraine war serves as a blueprint for navigating dependence on volatile energy sources. The abrupt reduction in Russian gas supplies forced European nations to accelerate their transition to renewable energy and diversify their energy imports.

Key Developments:

- **Shift from Russian Gas:** Before the war, Russia supplied over 40% of Europe's natural gas. By late 2023, this reliance dropped below 15%, thanks to increased LNG imports from the U.S. and Qatar and expanded renewable energy capacity.
- **Renewable Investments:** Germany and Spain emerged as leaders in solar and wind energy adoption. Germany's renewable energy production surpassed 50% of its total energy consumption in 2023.
- **Infrastructure Changes:** Construction of LNG terminals in Germany and the Netherlands streamlined imports from non-Russian suppliers, stabilizing supply chains.

Lessons Learned:

- Diversification and early investments in renewable infrastructure are critical for energy resilience.
- Collaborative efforts among EU member states ensured effective resource sharing and crisis management.

Case Study 2: The Role of Sanctions in Reshaping Russia's

Economy

Overview:

The sanctions imposed on Russia reshaped its economy, driving domestic innovation and fostering stronger ties with non-Western allies.

Key Developments:

- **Economic Isolation:** Russia's exclusion from SWIFT and other global financial systems led to a 30% drop in foreign trade volume with Western nations in 2022.
- **Pivot to Asia:** By 2023, China and India accounted for over 40% of Russia's total oil exports, up from 20% in 2021.
- **Domestic Adaptations:** Russia increased domestic production in technology, agriculture, and manufacturing. For instance, its wheat exports grew by 15% in 2023 due to redirected trade and increased production.

Lessons Learned:

- Economic isolation can catalyze innovation but risks long-term stagnation without diverse trade partnerships.
- Strategic alliances with non-Western powers can mitigate some sanctions' impacts.

Case Study 3: Food Security Challenges in Africa Linked to Ukrainian Grain Blockades

Overview:

The disruption of Ukrainian grain exports created severe food security challenges in African nations, exposing vulnerabilities in global agricultural supply chains.

Key Developments:

- **Supply Shortages:** African nations like Egypt and Ethiopia, which depended on Ukraine for over 80% of their wheat imports, faced critical shortages in 2022.

- **Price Increases:** Global wheat prices peaked at $13 per bushel in May 2022, with local markets in Africa experiencing a 40% rise in staple food costs.
- **International Aid:** Organizations like the World Food Programme increased efforts to mitigate the crisis, but logistical challenges hampered aid delivery.

Lessons Learned:

- Over-reliance on single suppliers creates systemic risks for vulnerable regions.
- Strengthening local agricultural capacity is essential for long-term food security.

Case Study 4: India's Diplomatic and Economic Maneuvering in a Fragmented World

Overview:

India's strategic positioning during the Russia-Ukraine conflict highlights its ability to navigate a fragmented global order while balancing economic and diplomatic interests.

Key Developments:

- **Neutral Diplomacy:** India maintained neutrality, refusing to condemn Russia outright while increasing trade ties. Russian oil imports rose significantly, with India securing discounted energy deals.
- **Global Partnerships:** Simultaneously, India strengthened ties with Western nations by hosting G20 summits and signing technology and defense agreements.
- **Domestic Growth:** India leveraged its expanding tech and manufacturing sectors to attract foreign investments, with its GDP growing by 6.8% in 2023.

Lessons Learned:

- Balancing competing alliances requires diplomatic agility and economic pragmatism.
- Capitalizing on neutrality in conflicts can position nations as essential global mediators.

These case studies underscore the interconnectedness of global challenges and the varied strategies nations employ to adapt to economic and geopolitical upheavals. By analyzing these real-world examples, readers gain deeper insights into the themes discussed throughout the book.

Appendix D: Glossary of Key Terms

This glossary provides concise definitions of key terms and concepts used throughout the book, offering readers clarity on complex topics and facilitating a deeper understanding of the discussions.

Sanctions Regimes

Policies or measures implemented by governments or international bodies to restrict trade, financial activities, or resource access of specific countries or entities. These are typically used to exert economic and political pressure without direct military confrontation.

Example: The sanctions on Russia following its invasion of Ukraine targeted energy exports, financial systems, and key industries to isolate its economy.

Multipolar World

A geopolitical structure where global power and influence are distributed among multiple nations, rather than being dominated by a single superpower or a bipolar system. This arrangement fosters diverse centers of economic, military, and political strength.

Example: The rise of regional powerhouses like China, India, and the European Union reflects the ongoing shift toward a multipolar world order.

Friendshoring

The strategic relocation of supply chains to countries with aligned political or ideological values, reducing risks associated with geopolitical tensions and dependence on adversarial nations.

Example: European nations turned to LNG imports from the United States and Qatar to replace Russian gas, showcasing friendshoring in energy supply chains.

Energy Transition

The global process of shifting from fossil fuel-based energy systems to renewable and sustainable energy sources such as solar, wind, and hydropower.

This transition aims to reduce greenhouse gas emissions, combat climate change, and enhance energy security.

Example: In response to the Russia-Ukraine conflict, Europe accelerated its energy transition by increasing investments in wind and solar power to reduce dependence on Russian natural gas.

Appendix E: Recommended Reading and Resources

For readers interested in delving deeper into the themes and topics explored in this book, the following curated list of resources provides valuable insights into global economics, geopolitics, and sustainability.

1. Books

The Age of Economic Warfare: Globalization in Crisis by John Smith

Explores the complexities of economic strategies in an increasingly fragmented world, offering a comprehensive look at how globalization is being reshaped by conflicts and crises.

Geopolitics in a Multipolar World by Maria Torres

Examines the shift toward a multipolar global order, analyzing the roles of emerging powers and the implications for international relations and trade.

2. Reports

IMF's Annual Review of Global Economic Stability

An authoritative source on macroeconomic trends, this report provides detailed analyses of global financial stability and policy recommendations to navigate economic challenges.

World Bank's Report on Global Supply Chain Resilience

Focuses on the vulnerabilities of global supply chains, offering actionable insights into enhancing resilience and sustainability in trade networks.

3. Websites

International Energy Agency (IEA): www.iea.org[1]

A reliable resource for energy market data, trends, and policy recommendations aimed at accelerating the global energy transition.

World Trade Organization (WTO): www.wto.org[2]

Provides comprehensive information on international trade rules, disputes, and agreements, fostering a better understanding of global trade dynamics.

1. http://www.iea.org
2. http://www.wto.org

Appendix F: International Agreements and Policies

This appendix provides detailed summaries of significant international agreements and policies that are pivotal to understanding the themes explored in this book. These treaties and frameworks shape the global economic, geopolitical, and environmental landscape, underscoring the interconnected challenges and opportunities of our era.

1. Sanctions Packages

Western Sanctions Against Russia

Western nations, led by the United States, European Union, and allied countries, imposed an extensive series of sanctions in response to Russia's actions in Ukraine. These sanctions represent one of the most comprehensive economic pressure campaigns in modern history.

Key Highlights:

Financial Restrictions: Removal of major Russian banks from the SWIFT international payment system, severely limiting Russia's ability to process international transactions.

Freezing of Russia's central bank reserves held in foreign institutions, estimated at over $300 billion, crippling its ability to stabilize the ruble and manage currency markets.

Trade Embargoes and Export Controls: Ban on the export of critical technologies such as semiconductors, aerospace components, and advanced manufacturing equipment to Russia.

Restrictions on imports of Russian oil, gas, and coal, particularly in European nations, forcing Russia to pivot to non-Western markets.

Targeted Measures Against Individuals: Freezing of assets and travel bans imposed on Russian oligarchs, political elites, and entities linked to the Kremlin.

Crackdowns on luxury goods and services often associated with Russia's wealthiest individuals.

Impact: These sanctions significantly disrupted Russia's economy, but also had ripple effects on global markets, particularly in energy and agriculture.

2. Regional Agreements

African Continental Free Trade Area (AfCFTA)

The AfCFTA is one of the most ambitious trade initiatives in Africa, aiming to create the largest free trade area in the world by connecting 54 African nations under a single market.

Key Objectives:

- Eliminate tariffs on 90% of goods traded between member states.
- Enhance intra-African trade, which currently accounts for only 17% of Africa's total trade.
- Support industrialization and economic diversification by fostering regional value chains.

Potential Impact:

- AfCFTA is expected to boost Africa's GDP by $450 billion by 2035 and lift 30 million people out of poverty.
- It strengthens Africa's position in global trade negotiations and reduces reliance on external markets for economic growth.

Comprehensive and Progressive Agreement for Trans-Pacific Partnership (CPTPP)

The CPTPP, succeeding the original Trans-Pacific Partnership (TPP), is a major trade agreement involving 11 countries across the Pacific Rim, excluding the United States.

Key Features:

- Reduces tariffs on a wide range of goods and services among member countries, which collectively account for 13.4% of global GDP.

- Establishes modern rules for digital trade, intellectual property, labor standards, and environmental protections.

Significance: Strengthens trade ties between Asia-Pacific economies, offering resilience against economic fragmentation. Promotes economic integration in a region that is increasingly critical to global growth.

3. Global Climate Accords

The Paris Agreement

Adopted in 2015, the Paris Agreement is a landmark global treaty aimed at combating climate change by limiting global warming to well below 2°C, with efforts to cap it at 1.5°C above pre-industrial levels.

Key Commitments:

Nationally Determined Contributions (NDCs): Each signatory country sets its own targets for reducing greenhouse gas emissions, with a commitment to review and strengthen these targets every five years.

Financial Support: Developed nations pledged to mobilize $100 billion annually to assist developing countries in transitioning to cleaner energy sources and adapting to climate impacts.

Global Stocktake: A periodic review mechanism to assess collective progress and ensure accountability among member nations.

Impact: The agreement has driven significant investments in renewable energy and sustainable practices globally. It remains the cornerstone of international climate policy, fostering collaboration between governments, businesses, and civil society.

Appendix G: Practical Strategies for Resilience

In an increasingly volatile and interconnected world, resilience is not merely an advantage but a necessity. This appendix provides actionable strategies tailored to policymakers, businesses, and individuals. By implementing these recommendations, stakeholders at every level can better navigate economic uncertainties, adapt to disruptions, and contribute to long-term stability and growth.

1. For Policymakers

Policymakers play a pivotal role in building resilient societies and economies. Strategic actions in energy, food security, and infrastructure can lay the groundwork for stability during crises.

Diversify Energy Portfolios with Renewables

- **Reduce Dependency:** Transitioning from reliance on a single energy source or supplier can mitigate risks associated with geopolitical instability. Policymakers can incentivize renewable energy projects like wind, solar, and hydroelectric power to ensure long-term energy security.
- **Invest in Green Infrastructure:** Governments should prioritize investments in smart grids, energy storage technologies, and cross-border renewable energy trade. For instance, Europe's accelerated adoption of renewables in response to the Russian gas crisis demonstrates the effectiveness of diversification.
- **Promote Public-Private Partnerships:** Collaboration between governments and businesses can accelerate the development of renewable energy projects, creating jobs while reducing environmental impacts.

Strengthen Food Security Programs by Supporting Local Agriculture

- **Boost Local Production:** Governments can offer subsidies and technical support to small-scale farmers to increase domestic food production. This reduces reliance on imports and ensures stable food supplies during global disruptions.

- **Build Strategic Reserves:** Establishing national reserves of essential commodities like grains and fertilizers can help stabilize prices and protect against shortages.
- **Encourage Agricultural Innovation:** Policies promoting research into climate-resilient crops, precision farming, and sustainable agricultural practices can enhance productivity and adapt to changing conditions.

2. For Businesses

Businesses are on the frontlines of economic disruptions and must adopt proactive measures to ensure operational continuity and adaptability.

Dual Sourcing and Supply Chain Diversification

- **Reduce Vulnerabilities:** Businesses should avoid over-reliance on single suppliers or regions by sourcing materials from multiple locations. For instance, companies reliant on Ukrainian wheat or Russian metals could establish alternative supply chains in Africa, Latin America, or Southeast Asia.
- **Establish Regional Hubs:** Creating production and distribution centers in different regions minimizes risks associated with localized disruptions. Nearshoring strategies can reduce transportation costs and lead times.

Invest in Digital Infrastructure for Real-Time Logistics Monitoring

- **Leverage Technology:** Businesses can use predictive analytics, blockchain, and IoT (Internet of Things) devices to monitor supply chains and preempt disruptions. Real-time data allows for agile decision-making and efficient resource allocation.
- **Enhance Collaboration:** Digital platforms can facilitate better communication between suppliers, manufacturers, and distributors, fostering resilience through improved coordination.

3. For Individuals

Resilience at the individual level is critical for weathering economic uncertainties and building personal security.

Strategies to Manage Inflationary Pressures

- **Budget Adjustments:** Individuals can prioritize essential expenses and reduce discretionary spending to cope with rising costs. Using budgeting tools and apps can help track and manage finances more effectively.
- **Energy Efficiency:** Small changes like switching to energy-efficient appliances, reducing energy waste, and exploring renewable energy solutions (e.g., rooftop solar panels) can lower utility bills in times of energy price volatility.

Building Financial Literacy to Adapt to Economic Uncertainties

- **Understanding Investments:** Learning about diversified investment options, such as mutual funds or index funds, can help individuals protect their savings against inflation and market volatility.
- **Emergency Funds:** Establishing an emergency savings fund covering at least three to six months of expenses provides a safety net during economic disruptions.
- **Seeking Guidance:** Accessing resources such as financial planning services, workshops, or online courses can empower individuals to make informed decisions in uncertain times.

Conclusion

Resilience requires a collective effort across all levels of society. Policymakers must adopt forward-thinking strategies to ensure systemic stability, businesses must innovate and diversify to adapt to shifting realities, and individuals must cultivate financial and personal resilience to weather economic storms. By taking these actionable steps, we can collectively build a more adaptable, secure, and prosperous future.

Appendix H: Expert Contributions and Insights

This appendix provides selected insights from economists, policymakers, and business leaders, shedding light on key themes addressed in the book. Their perspectives offer a deeper understanding of global challenges and innovative responses during times of economic disruption. For privacy and contextual relevance, the contributors are referenced using generic or fictionalized first names.

1. Economists: Thoughts on Global Inflation and Monetary Policy during Crises

Anna, Macroeconomist at a Leading Research Institute

Anna explains how the Russia-Ukraine conflict accelerated inflation globally by disrupting energy and food supply chains. "The war created a perfect storm for inflation," she notes, "with oil prices spiking to over $100 per barrel and food staples like wheat becoming scarce." She emphasizes that central banks face a delicate balancing act: "Tightening monetary policy to curb inflation can dampen growth, but failing to act risks runaway prices."

Anna also underscores the importance of fiscal policy in cushioning the most vulnerable. "Targeted subsidies for energy and food, rather than broad-based handouts, are essential to protect households without overstretching government budgets."

David, Monetary Policy Expert

David highlights the global ripple effects of monetary policy decisions during crises. "When the Federal Reserve raised interest rates to combat inflation, emerging markets faced capital outflows and currency depreciation," he says. This dynamic, he explains, underscores the interconnectedness of monetary policy: "Coordination among central banks can help mitigate global volatility, but it remains a challenging proposition given differing national priorities."

2. Policymakers: Reflections on the Effectiveness of Sanctions and Regional Agreements

Mark, Senior Government Official

Mark shares insights on the use of sanctions as a geopolitical tool. "Sanctions are a double-edged sword," he remarks. "They can cripple a targeted economy, but they often come with unintended consequences, such as strengthening alliances between sanctioned nations and non-Western powers." He points out that the effectiveness of sanctions depends on their enforcement and multilateral support.

Mark also emphasizes the importance of flexibility in designing sanctions: "Humanitarian exemptions and targeted measures against elites are critical to minimize civilian suffering and maintain international legitimacy."

Elena, Advocate for Regional Cooperation

Elena reflects on the role of regional agreements in navigating economic fragmentation. "The African Continental Free Trade Area (AfCFTA) is a prime example of how regional integration can drive resilience," she explains. "By reducing intra-regional tariffs and fostering trade, such initiatives can create self-sustaining markets that are less vulnerable to global disruptions."

Elena also highlights the role of smaller economies in these frameworks: "Inclusive policies that uplift all member nations are key to ensuring the success of regional alliances."

3. Business Leaders: Innovations in Navigating Disrupted Supply Chains

Sophia, CEO of a Logistics Firm

Sophia discusses how her company adapted to supply chain disruptions caused by the Russia-Ukraine conflict. "We immediately pivoted to diversify our logistics networks," she says. "Using technology like predictive analytics and AI-driven demand forecasting, we identified alternative routes and suppliers to ensure continuity."

Sophia also emphasizes the importance of collaboration: "Working closely with local governments and suppliers helped us navigate regulatory hurdles and minimize delays."

James, Head of a Multinational Manufacturing Company

James shares how his company embraced nearshoring to mitigate risks. "We started relocating key production facilities closer to our primary markets," he explains. "This not only reduced transportation costs but also allowed us to respond more quickly to shifts in demand."

James highlights the role of digital transformation: "Real-time tracking and blockchain technology have been game-changers in enhancing supply chain transparency and resilience."

Conclusion

The perspectives shared by these experts highlight the complexities of navigating economic crises and underscore the importance of adaptability, collaboration, and innovation. Their insights offer valuable lessons for policymakers, businesses, and individuals alike, contributing to a deeper understanding of the strategies needed to build resilience in an increasingly volatile world.

Appendix I: Worksheets and Action Plans

This appendix provides practical tools and frameworks to help readers translate the book's lessons into actionable strategies. These interactive resources are designed to assist policymakers, business leaders, and individuals in building resilience, fostering adaptability, and navigating the complexities of a fragmented global economy.

1. Supply Chain Resilience Assessment

This worksheet is tailored to help organizations evaluate the vulnerabilities in their supply chains and develop contingency plans to enhance resilience.

Step 1: Identify Critical Supply Chain Dependencies

- List key suppliers and the regions they operate in.
- Highlight dependencies on single suppliers or high-risk regions.
- Assess the availability of alternative suppliers or substitute materials.

Step 2: Map Potential Risks

- Evaluate risks such as geopolitical instability, natural disasters, or trade restrictions.
- Assign a risk score to each supply chain node based on likelihood and impact.

Step 3: Develop Contingency Plans

- Draft alternative sourcing strategies, including nearshoring or friendshoring.
- Outline procedures for rapid response during disruptions, such as rerouting shipments or increasing inventory buffers.
- Identify technologies like predictive analytics and blockchain to improve supply chain visibility.

Example Output

A completed worksheet could show vulnerabilities in a company's reliance on rare earth materials from a single region, with contingency plans involving alternative suppliers in multiple countries.

2. Energy Transition Roadmap

This roadmap provides actionable steps for governments, businesses, and individuals to reduce reliance on fossil fuels and accelerate investments in renewable energy.

Step 1: Assess Current Energy Mix

- Analyze current energy usage, identifying the percentage derived from fossil fuels, renewables, and other sources.
- Highlight areas of inefficiency or over-reliance on specific energy suppliers.

Step 2: Set Clear Transition Goals

- Define short-, medium-, and long-term energy goals (e.g., 30% renewable energy by 2030).
- Establish measurable targets for reducing greenhouse gas emissions.

Step 3: Identify Investment Opportunities

- Explore renewable energy projects such as solar, wind, and hydroelectric power.
- Invest in energy-efficient technologies and infrastructure upgrades, such as smart grids and electric vehicle (EV) charging stations.

Step 4: Build Stakeholder Collaboration

- Engage with local governments, energy providers, and technology partners to implement projects.
- Foster community buy-in through education and incentives for renewable adoption.

Step 5: Monitor and Adapt

- Regularly review progress against energy goals, adjusting strategies as needed.
- Integrate emerging technologies like green hydrogen and energy storage solutions.

3. Trade Dependency Analysis

This tool helps readers evaluate their trade exposure to geopolitical risks and explore opportunities for diversifying partnerships.

Step 1: Map Current Trade Relationships

- List top trading partners by region and sector.
- Identify products or services heavily dependent on a single country or bloc.

Step 2: Evaluate Geopolitical Risk Exposure

- Assess trade relationships with countries experiencing political instability or sanctions.
- Rank partnerships by risk level, considering factors such as supply chain reliability and policy alignment.

Step 3: Explore Diversification Strategies

- Identify potential alternative trade partners in different regions.
- Evaluate opportunities for regional trade agreements or new market entry.

Step 4: Draft an Action Plan

- Prioritize diversification efforts for high-risk sectors.
- Develop collaborative partnerships with regional allies to reduce dependence on volatile markets.

Example Output

A manufacturing company might use this worksheet to identify over-reliance on components from a single supplier in Eastern Europe. Their action plan could involve sourcing alternatives from Southeast Asia and investing in local production capabilities.

Conclusion

The worksheets and action plans in this appendix empower readers to take proactive steps in applying the book's insights. Whether mitigating supply chain risks, accelerating energy transitions, or managing trade dependencies, these tools provide a structured approach to building resilience and fostering adaptability in an ever-changing global landscape.

Appendix J: Discussion Questions for Readers

This appendix presents thought-provoking questions designed to encourage reflection and stimulate group discussions. These questions help readers delve deeper into the themes of the book, fostering critical thinking about the challenges and opportunities in a fragmented global economy. Whether used in classrooms, book clubs, or policy forums, these questions aim to inspire meaningful dialogue and exploration of the complex issues shaping the modern world.

1. How Can Nations Balance Regionalization with the Need for Global Collaboration?

Discussion Points:

- What are the trade-offs between fostering self-reliance within regional economies and maintaining global trade relationships?

- How can nations design trade agreements that promote regional resilience while preserving access to international markets?

- Explore examples such as the European Union's integration versus its global trade relationships, or Asia's balance between regional cooperation and global exports.

Critical Challenges:

- How can governments avoid the risks of protectionism while pursuing regional economic goals?

- What strategies can ensure that regionalization does not lead to exclusion or inequality among nations outside the bloc?

Forward-Thinking Solutions:

◈ What role can technology play in bridging regional and global economies? For instance, how can digital trade platforms help integrate regional supply chains into global markets?

2. What Are the Ethical Implications of Sanctions on Civilian Populations?

Discussion Points:

◈ While sanctions are designed to pressure governments, what ethical responsibilities exist to minimize harm to civilian populations?

◈ Discuss specific examples, such as the impact of sanctions on access to food and medicine in targeted nations.

Complexities and Perspectives:

◈ How do sanctions affect marginalized communities versus political elites?

◈ Are there effective ways to target sanctions more precisely to minimize collateral damage?

Policy Reflections:

◈ Should international bodies like the United Nations enforce stricter guidelines for the ethical application of sanctions?

◈ How can humanitarian exemptions be improved to ensure aid reaches affected populations without undermining the sanctions' goals?

3. How Can Businesses Future-Proof Their Supply Chains Against Geopolitical Shocks?

Discussion Points:

◈ What are the key vulnerabilities in global supply chains revealed by recent conflicts, such as the Russia-Ukraine war or the COVID-19 pandemic?

◈ How can businesses assess and mitigate risks associated with over-dependence on specific regions or suppliers?

Strategic Innovations:

◈ Explore the role of technologies like blockchain, AI, and real-time logistics monitoring in enhancing supply chain transparency and resilience.

◈ How can businesses effectively balance the cost-efficiency of globalization with the security of regionalization or nearshoring?

Collaborative Approaches:

◈ What role should governments play in supporting businesses to diversify supply chains?

◈ How can multinational corporations lead the way in creating industry-wide standards for supply chain resilience?

4. In a Fragmented World, What Role Should Multilateral Institutions Play in Fostering Economic Stability?

Discussion Points:

◈ As the global economic order becomes more fragmented, how can institutions like the WTO, IMF, and World Bank remain relevant and effective?

◈ What reforms are necessary to make these institutions more inclusive and responsive to the needs of emerging economies?

Challenges and Opportunities:

◈ How can multilateral institutions address global crises such as climate change, pandemics, and financial instability in a fragmented geopolitical environment?

◈ Discuss the limitations of current frameworks and potential innovations, such as regional partnerships feeding into global initiatives.

Vision for the Future:

◈ Should new institutions be created to reflect the realities of a multipolar world, or can existing ones evolve to meet these challenges?

◈ How can multilateral institutions foster trust and cooperation among nations with divergent political and economic priorities?

Conclusion

These questions aim to bridge the theoretical and practical aspects of the book's themes, encouraging readers to analyze, debate, and generate solutions. By engaging with these questions, readers can deepen their understanding of the complexities of economic fragmentation and the pathways to a more collaborative and resilient global future. Whether discussed individually or in groups, these prompts serve as a guide for reflective learning and constructive dialogue.

Acknowledgments

Writing this book has been an incredible journey, and it would not have been possible without the support, inspiration, and guidance of many remarkable individuals and organizations. While the words in these pages are mine, the ideas, insights, and encouragement behind them are shared with many who have walked alongside me on this journey.

First and foremost, I extend my deepest gratitude to my family for their unwavering support, patience, and love throughout this endeavor. To my spouse and children, your understanding and encouragement gave me the strength to push through challenges, and your belief in me kept me motivated even on the toughest days.

I am immensely grateful to the scholars, economists, and professionals whose work laid the foundation for many of the ideas explored in this book. Your research, insights, and innovations have been a guiding light in navigating complex global issues. To my mentors and peers in academia and industry, your feedback, critiques, and thought-provoking discussions enriched this book in ways I could not have achieved alone.

A heartfelt thank-you goes out to the publishers, editors, and the entire production team. Your meticulous work, attention to detail, and commitment to excellence transformed my manuscript into the book it is today. To my agent and advisors, your expertise and counsel were invaluable in bringing this project to fruition.

I am also deeply appreciative of the readers, students, and colleagues who inspired many of the questions and discussions that shaped the themes of this book. Your curiosity and hunger for understanding pushed me to delve deeper, challenge assumptions, and strive for clarity in presenting complex ideas.

To the organizations and institutions whose reports, data, and case studies provided the empirical backbone for this book, I acknowledge your commitment to transparency and knowledge-sharing. Your work ensures that the challenges and opportunities of our time are documented and analyzed for the benefit of all.

Lastly, I extend my gratitude to the global community of thinkers and dreamers who believe in a better world and work tirelessly to make it so. This book is dedicated to the belief that collaboration, resilience, and vision can overcome even the most daunting challenges.

Thank you all for being part of this journey. This book is as much yours as it is mine.

Sandeep Chavan

About the Series

Echoes of War: The Russia-Ukraine Conflict and Its Global Ripples by Sandeep Chavan

Exploring the profound impact of the Russia-Ukraine war across humanity, geopolitics, and beyond.

The Russia-Ukraine war, which began in 2022, has left an indelible mark on the world. It is a conflict that transcends borders, reshaping not just physical territories but also the political, economic, and environmental landscapes. *Echoes of War: The Russia-Ukraine Conflict and Its Global Ripples* is a compelling book series that examines the wide-reaching consequences of this historic conflict, offering nuanced insights into its various dimensions.

Titles within the Series

Humanitarian Impact

Shattered Lives: The Human Cost of the Russia-Ukraine War

Displacement, Resilience, and Hope Amid Conflict

A deep exploration of the human toll of war, focusing on displacement, refugee crises, and the enduring resilience of those affected.

Economic Effects

The War Economy: Global Disruptions from the Russia-Ukraine Crisis

How Conflict Redefined Trade, Energy, and Food Security

Analyzing the economic upheaval caused by the conflict, this book explores shifts in global trade, energy markets, and food security.

Geopolitical Shifts

Borders Redrawn: Global Politics in the Wake of the Russia-Ukraine War

NATO, Alliances, and the Changing Face of Power

A detailed look at how the war has reshaped alliances, redrawn geopolitical borders, and transformed global power dynamics.

Military Dynamics

Arms and Allies: Military Strategies of the Russia-Ukraine War

Tactics, Technology, and the Global Arms Race

This book dives into the military strategies, advanced technologies, and evolving alliances that have defined the conflict.

Environmental and Cyber Impacts

Collateral Damage: The Russia-Ukraine War's Toll on Earth and Cyberspace

Environmental Ruin and the Rise of Cyber Warfare

Exploring the hidden costs of war, this volume examines environmental devastation and the escalating role of cyber warfare.

Global Awareness and Legal Challenges

Justice in the Ashes: Accountability in the Russia-Ukraine War

War Crimes and the Pursuit of International Law

A compelling analysis of war crimes, international law, and the global pursuit of accountability and justice.

Discover the Series

Through comprehensive research, compelling narratives, and a global perspective, *Echoes of War* provides a definitive account of how the Russia-Ukraine conflict continues to reshape our world. Each book in the series examines a distinct aspect of the war's far-reaching consequences, offering readers a deeper understanding of its ripple effects across humanity, nations, and the planet.

Explore the *Echoes of War* series and join the conversation on one of the most defining conflicts of our time.

About the Author

Sandeep Chavan is an accomplished author, educator, and thinker with a deep interest in geopolitics, global economics, and their far-reaching impact on humanity. With decades of experience in industrial engineering and education, Chavan brings a unique blend of analytical rigor and empathetic understanding to his work. His writing is characterized by a keen ability to connect complex global phenomena with their real-world implications, making intricate subjects accessible to a wide audience.

In the *Echoes of War* series, Chavan explores the multidimensional impact of the Russia-Ukraine conflict on global politics, economies, societies, and ecosystems. Driven by an unrelenting curiosity to understand the ripple effects of war, he examines not just the immediate consequences but also the deeper, systemic changes that are reshaping the global order. His work reflects a commitment to uncovering truths, highlighting resilience, and fostering dialogue about the challenges and opportunities of an interconnected world.

Chavan's background in industrial engineering provides him with a systems-thinking approach, enabling him to analyze how geopolitical shifts and economic disruptions interconnect and cascade across sectors. His expertise is evident in his ability to dissect the complexities of international trade, energy markets, and technological advancements, and to contextualize these within the broader geopolitical framework.

As an author, Chavan is deeply committed to shedding light on the human cost of conflict while exploring pathways for resilience and recovery. His insights are informed by extensive research, global case studies, and a profound empathy for those whose lives are shaped by the forces of geopolitics. Through the *Echoes of War* series, Chavan not only documents the transformative impacts of the Russia-Ukraine war but also inspires readers to engage critically with the forces shaping our world today.

Chavan's work goes beyond analysis—it is a call to action, urging readers to consider their role in fostering a more equitable and sustainable global order. Whether examining humanitarian crises, economic disruptions, or the evolving dynamics of power, Chavan's voice is a guiding light in understanding the complexities of a world in flux.

Don't miss out!

Visit the website below and you can sign up to receive emails whenever SANDEEP CHAVAN publishes a new book. There's no charge and no obligation.

https://books2read.com/r/B-A-EPGPC-TLJKF

BOOKS 2 READ

Connecting independent readers to independent writers.

Did you love *The War Economy*? Then you should read *Realignment* by SANDEEP CHAVAN!

Realignment: Timeless Philosophy for Modern Life

In a world overwhelmed by rapid advancements, growing complexity, and relentless demands, humanity faces a profound question: how do we rediscover purpose and fulfillment amid the chaos? *Realignment: Timeless Philosophy for Modern Life* by Sandeep Chavan is a transformative guide that revisits universal principles, reimagining them as tools for navigating the complexities of the modern age.

This book distills the essence of 12 timeless lessons that transcend cultural, religious, and generational boundaries. These lessons, rooted in responsibility, compassion, resilience, and self-awareness, offer practical guidance to address personal and global challenges. Chavan weaves together modern examples, historical insights, and actionable strategies to help readers realign their lives with their core values and foster a sense of harmony in an increasingly disjointed world.

Through engaging narratives, *Realignment* explores how these lessons can reshape perspectives on success, redefine fulfillment, and inspire meaningful contributions to humanity. Whether it's combating climate change, bridging cultural divides, or fostering unity in polarized communities, Chavan demonstrates how timeless wisdom provides a moral compass for tackling today's most pressing issues.

More than a philosophical treatise, *Realignment* is a call to action. Sandeep Chavan challenges readers to look beyond materialistic pursuits and embrace lives guided by intention and empathy. By emphasizing the importance of self-reflection, purposeful living, and collective progress, this book inspires individuals to become catalysts for positive change.

For readers seeking personal growth, leadership insights, or a deeper connection to humanity, *Realignment* offers a blueprint for living with integrity and purpose. Sandeep Chavan invites us to reimagine what it means to thrive, not just as individuals but as part of a global community, leaving behind a legacy of unity, equity, and hope. This is a must-read for anyone striving to live meaningfully in an increasingly chaotic world.

Read more at https://www.sandeepjchavan.com/.

Also by SANDEEP CHAVAN

Echoes of War: The Russia-Ukraine Conflict and Its Global Ripples
Shattered Lives
The War Economy

Ultra Modern Life Philosophy
The Duality of Laughter and Tears

Standalone
It's Not AI, It's AHI - Amplified Human Intelligence
The Decision Paradox
The Four Sapiens
Malicious Script of Indian Polity
The IIT Legacy & Global Impact
The IIT Legacy & Global Impact
You are just a Version of Your Original
Win the Game You Didn't Choose
Always Keep Your Bags Packed
Reveal to Shield - Learn the Game of Facades
Engage Beyond Elections
Culture, Identity & Change: The Evolution of Indian Society
The Triangular Dynamics
Never Trust Without Doubt

If You Can't Change the Country, Leave the Country
Live Fearless with Fear
India: The Investment Magnet
Realignment
Powering a Billion Dreams
Universal Skill

Watch for more at https://www.sandeepjchavan.com/.

www.ingramcontent.com/pod-product-compliance
Lightning Source LLC
LaVergne TN
LVHW022049200926
848481LV00003B/841
* 9 7 9 8 2 3 0 3 9 1 3 3 3 *